PENGUIN BOOKS

THE ANATOMY OF A STING

Bhupen Patel has been editor (crime and investigations) for *Mid-Day* since August 2011. He has served as special correspondent, assistant editor, crime editor and editor (investigations) at different news publications, such as the *Daily* and *Mumbai Mirror* over the last eighteen years. He also worked as special correspondent with NDTV 24x7. Investigations have been his core focus, and he has several exclusive stories to his credit, including cracking the modus of the Mumbai blasts in 2006 and receiving exclusive access to Ajmal Kasab's interrogation CD, which made it to the front page of *Mumbai Mirror* and was telecast by all news channels.

THE ANATOMY OF A STING

AN INSIDE LOOK INTO UNDERCOVER OPERATIONS

BHUPEN PATEL

PENGUIN BOOKS

An imprint of Penguin Random House

PENGUIN BOOKS

USA | Canada | UK | Ireland | Australia
New Zealand | India | South Africa | China | Singapore

Penguin Books is part of the Penguin Random House group of companies
whose addresses can be found at global.penguinrandomhouse.com

Published by Penguin Random House India Pvt. Ltd
4th Floor, Capital Tower 1, MG Road,
Gurugram 122 002, Haryana, India

Penguin
Random House
India

First published in Penguin Books by Blue Salt Media and
Penguin Random House India 2018

ISBN 9780143441762

Typeset in Adobe Caslon Pro by Manipal Digital Systems, Manipal

Printed at Repro India Limited

www.penguin.co.in

FOREWORD

Had the two intrepid journalists from the *Washington Post*, Bob Woodward and Carl Bernstein, not relentlessly pursued the leads they got from a source they called 'Deep Throat', the world would perhaps not have come to know the full extent of the Watergate scandal that cost Richard Nixon his presidency in 1972. In the past century or so, there have been many path-breaking investigative stories that changed the political landscapes of their countries. Closer home, the Bofors scandal—exposed after the Swedish Radio broke the story of kickbacks in the Rs 1437-crore Bofors howitzer deal—changed the political landscape of India in 1989. Needless to say, the country has produced some of the finest investigative journalists who have exposed crimes and corruption in public life.

As you leaf through the pages of *The Anatomy of a Sting*, you will come across tales of grit, gore and grime from the world of crime. These tales, told with all their grey shades, force you to hold your breath, wondering how the journalist pulled off these coups, sometimes putting his team and himself in mortal danger.

But then journalism is no cakewalk. A journalist has to follow the basics—who, what, why, where, when, how—while pursuing a lead or a story idea. Although all stories, even if they are mundane, require due diligence, investigative journalism requires talent, skill, money and luck. An accountant and a lawyer should not be allowed to have a say before an assignment is complete. An investigative journalist, like me, gets a kick only when an undertaking is accomplished and he breaks the story. As a journalist, if a story does not enthuse you or thrill you, you cease to be a serious muckraker!

For you to crack a story, well, you need adequate planning. This entails cross-checking the facts, budgeting a proposed investigation and working out the pros and cons of every move, including when to exit the scene unscathed if things get too hot to handle. The source is the key to a good lead and needs to be protected at all costs. It may take months for a story to reach its logical conclusion. In case a hidden camera is used when there is no other recourse, a journalist has to get into the skin of the character he is investigating. Apart from these basic ingredients, there has to be a risk analysis in case the journalist is caught with the camera. If his life is in danger, it is judicious to call off the operation at once.

A story narrated in this book exemplifies the risks involved. As it happened, the journalist pursued a tip-off after twin bomb blasts, one in Zaveri Bazaar and the other at Gateway of India, shook Mumbai in August 2003. After making inquiries with the investigating authorities, it was clear that there was more to the story than met the eye. The operation was undertaken to nail the mastermind behind the blasts, who was ensconced in Dubai, although the man who had executed the blasts had been arrested along with his wife, his accomplice. Pursuing a lead, the journalist went to Dubai but landed in a lock-up. In his zeal, the journalist discarded the cardinal principle of undercover investigation: play it discreet. He had to return to India as soon as the Dubai police let him off. Fortunately, his cover was not blown.

Although there are no fixed rules, for it all depends on the circumstances which may take unexpected turns to test your patience or shock you out of your wits, we at Cobrapost follow certain guidelines which every journalist should adhere to.

We are a country of dreamers. Many of us, especially when we are young, are smitten by the Bollywood bug! But very often, many of those starry-eyed youngsters end up being fleeced by conmen on the prowl who lay intricate traps to entice them with roles in films that never materialize. A journalist exposed two such conmen, who with the help of a Bollywood actor, had set up shop to con gullible dreamers. His expose on a mental asylum, showing how easy it was to throw someone hale and hearty into it, reminds me of a similar expose in nineteenth-century New York by the gutsy Nellie Bly, an undercover reporter who spent time in an asylum to tell the world how a perfectly sane person could easily make it to the house of the lunatics and the pathetic conditions prevailing there.

It was a coincidence when the sobbing eleven-year-old Ameena Begum, accompanied by an elderly Arab, caught the attention of an air hostess who raised an alarm. The next morning, in October 1991, the entire nation woke up to the shocking news of poor, underage girls being sold off in marriage to wealthy Arabs. The author also busted one such racket in Mumbai where rich Arabs on a pleasure trip to India married girls of their choice for as measly a sum as Rs 14,000, and after a week or two pronounced triple talaq before boarding a home-bound flight. However, the kingpin of this marriage-for-sex ring, a Mumbai qazi, and his accomplices vanished before the police swung into action. Sadly, such rackets still thrive both in Hyderabad and in Mumbai.

The stories that Bhupen Patel has knitted in this book are his labour of love during his stints with *Mid-Day*, *Mumbai Mirror* and NDTV, all in the city that never sleeps, the city which is called India's financial and business capital, the city which is host to the world's largest film industry, and the city which breeds crimes and criminals as effortlessly as it harbours a multitude of humanity of every imaginable colour, race and faith. Bhupen now heads the crime team at *Mid-Day*.

If criminals, racketeers and scamsters abound in our country, so do hard-boiled journalists who sniff out stories and are ready to expose all shady activities in public interest. And then there are journalists who share their dangerous yet fascinating journeys with their readers. This book is all about that.

Aniruddha Bahal
Founder and editor, Cobrapost

INTRODUCTION

Often, conventional and formulaic ways are not sufficient to tell a story. In fact, reporters will vouch for the fact that the more complex and intricate the assignment, the more thrilling and exciting the ride. Sometimes a straightforward approach is not enough to uncover the web of lies and deceit behind a story. Sometimes a journalist has to shatter the conspiracy of silence with a bang and, in the unmasking, he or she might have to walk a tightrope to bridge the distance in an unsavoury manner. Stings are not popular among all journalists, but I feel that for great stories one has to keep reservations on the matter aside and just take the plunge.

One case study is better than a thousand theories, hence the book in your hand. Here's a brief background for the uninitiated. During my stint at Somaiya College of Journalism in Mumbai's Vidyavihar, where I taught for three years, I emphasized on one cardinal principle: In journalism, remember that we emulate the example of Krishna and not Rama. Krishna's philosophy was highly controversial yet crystal clear. The end is important and not the means. Had Krishna not adhered to this principle, the Pandavas would never have won the battle and would have suffered a crushing and humiliating defeat at the hands of the Kauravas instead.

Greedy politicians, corrupt police top brass, incompetent and conniving bureaucrats, exploitative businessmen, land sharks and ruthless builders, lobbyists and fake godmen can never be exposed through traditional methods of reporting that have been practiced since the days of Narad Muni. Maneck Davar in the late 1980s changed the definition of Indian journalism with the hidden tape recorder. Aniruddha Bahal of Cobrapost went a step further and used the hidden camera. Aniruddha is totally fearless and has done some sensational candid camera, proving the effectiveness of this reporting style.

When *Mumbai Mirror* was launched on 30 May 2005, editor Meenal Baghel's brief was clear: Only exclusive and unique stories for the front page.

This was quite challenging and daunting. I suggested we cultivate a team of reporters to focus only on special investigations and that they be spared the responsibilities of routine reporting. Meenal, who was always game for a good challenge, agreed and allocated five reporters to the team, which included Bhupen Patel and Danish Khan, both of whom are now Blue Salt authors, ably supported by Naveeta Singh and later Ruhi Khan. I knew Bhupen since the time we had both worked at *Mid-Day*.

We worked on two fundamentals: We would never allow the newspaper to be used to further the agenda of our sources and that no fear or favour would decide the story.

Apart from these, we were willing to work around the rules to achieve our goal. It was a different era where journalism meant integrity. There were a few bad apples even then, but the loftiness of the profession was not dimmed. I will keep saying this that a motivated, uncompromising and honest journalist is an asset to society, second only to a scrupulous doctor.

The freedom to break any barrier to be able to achieve the team's goal without compromising on our principles went on to make *Mumbai Mirror* a success story. Our team managed to use every tool in its arsenal to break the defense of the wicked. We worked for fourteen hours a day to penetrate the dark underbelly of the city.

At the end, our sting operations resulted in path-breaking stories. We told stories of mental asylums that labelled a healthy and sane woman as insane, we exposed a gang of women buying babies for cash and selling them to childless couples, we spoke about the loophole in the system where criminals lodged in jails can prolong their stay in state-run hospitals after getting a medical certificate from J.J. Hospital. We discovered that the security at the MLA hostel at Nariman Point was porous like a railway station. You could walk in and stay there without anybody noticing. Bhupen had walked into a room there and spent three days without anybody raising an eyebrow.

The series of sting operations in *Mumbai Mirror* changed the face of journalism. In the last eighteen years, I have seen Bhupen grow professionally right from *Mid-Day*, to *Mumbai Mirror* to NDTV, to *Mumbai Mirror* and then back to *Mid-Day*, coming a full circle. He has been rock solid and epitomizes what a crime journalist should be.

I wanted Bhupen to write about his adventures. Some of them were hugely successful, some fell flat, while others had to be abandoned despite incriminating evidence. Nonetheless, the whole exercise of the operation is a lesson in journalism.

As a journalist who made his mark in crime journalism, I take pride in presenting this book to the readers. These ten stories are full of the excitement and rollercoaster rides that I am sure most reporters have felt at least once in their career.

Now, fasten your seat belts, you are about to take off!

S. Hussain Zaidi
author and journalist

ONE

'Aap dono perfect hain hero–heroine ke liye, ab bas phillam sign karne ki der hai. Isssmile now' (Both of you are perfect as the hero–heroine. Smile now), said a man sitting across the table, flashing his gutkha-stained teeth. 'I am signing you as the leads,' he added.

This is how I bagged my first Bollywood film, 'Pyaar Ki Aakhiri Manzil'. In fact, not just one, but two films. A mainstream commercial cinema and the other, an 'art' film, based on nuclear war. 'Woh dusra phillam toh ekdam "Ass-kur" ke liye ban raha hai.' I took a while to understand that he meant 'Oscar'. In this ten by ten square foot office, which its resident had 'painted' red by spitting gutkha everywhere, my colleague and I were offered to play the leads in two movies, on a mezzanine floor of Mumbai's Industrial hub at Andheri–Ghatkopar Link Road. 'Meet me tomorrow, I will keep the contract ready.'

This would be a dream beginning in Bollywood for countless struggling actors, but for me, it was the perfect end to my sting operation.

A Week Earlier, December 2006

The office of *Mumbai Mirror*

Times of India Building

Opposite Chhatrapati Shivaji Maharaj Terminus, Mumbai

It was another day of dealing with the stress of working at a newspaper. Get an exclusive, find the lead, make a list, assign photographers, check the police control room . . . and so it went on every day. It wasn't unusual to have the resident editor, Pankaj Upadhyaya, come over urgently to ask about our work either. His anxiety usually rose towards the end of every day. But this time he hadn't come to ask for anything. Instead, he wanted to give me a lead.

He pointed at a small classified in a Hindi weekly newspaper and said, 'Go for this.' Wondering what had caught Pankaj's eye on the corner of an inside page, I spotted an ad from Saathi Film International that said 'Fresher may apply' for the lead in a Bollywood film. I blushed at the thought that my boss believed I was suited to be a film star, before being told that he wanted me to check if this was a genuine call for actors. He pointed at Ruhi Khan, a year-old inclusion in the crime team and said, 'Decide if you want to be her casting agent or a friend.' Ruhi had returned from London, had a great sense of fashion and the perfect personality to be my partner for this mission. Before Pankaj could reach his cabin I heard him say, 'Deliver it in a week.'

In seven days, I was expected to deliver a 2,000 word article from a hunch about a four-line classified, without any lead, logistics or clarity. I wondered if Pankaj was confident or overconfident about my abilities. Not that I had a choice. So, I went.

The Recce

To us, a sting operation is nothing less than a police investigation. The difference is that reporters learn on the job without any specific training. Also, we rarely have backup and definitely don't have arms for self-defence.

I decided to do some groundwork first and stepped out to check if the address provided in the classified ad was legitimate. Since I would be accompanied by a female colleague and it would just be the two of us, it was important to have an idea of the surroundings, the number of people there and the escape routes.

I visited the office of Saathi Film International, located on the mezzanine floor of one of the industrial units of Anis Compound on the Andheri–Ghatkopar Link Road, a hub of small-scale industries in Mumbai. The ground floor had a few auto garages and spare parts shops. I was not surprised that the office did not have any nameplates or boards. From the dust on the shutters, it looked as though the premises had been shut for over a month. Apart from the door, a window was the only escape route from that small office.

I made inquiries with the staff of some of the shops in the locality but no one had a clue about the production house. A few things seemed clear to me—the company had hired the office just a few days ago and seemed highly suspect. It was unlikely that they would rent an office in this area, which didn't have the remotest ties with Bollywood.

Without any assistance or support from authorities, I wasn't sure if the story was worth following up. But when I reported back to office, I realized I had to give it a shot.

The Virtual Spy

Once we decided to go ahead with the story, the next important decision was to pick our third and most important partner: the hidden camera. Back then, spy cameras were relatively new, unlike now when the city's electronic stores on Lamington Road/DB Marg have a whole range at various prices. One can buy spy cameras for Rs 1500–2000, hidden in buttons, spectacles, watches, ties, etc. The 'Made in China' cameras can easily pull off three or four assignments without any glitches. But ten years ago, there was very little choice. The products available were of inferior quality, and the better cameras had a lot of wiring and were tough to carry on your person.

I was reminded of a senior reporter friend's experience. He had been on a sting operation about bribes taken by policemen, and just when his assignment was about to end, his camera had betrayed him. He put his hand in his pocket to remove cash but unfortunately unplugged the wires from the batteries, which popped out from his shirt. Since spy cameras were not as popular then, luckily for him, the officer bought his theory that he had unplugged the batteries of his hearing machine. I had to make sure I didn't repeat this mistake.

The Pre-Production

As a team, it was important for Ruhi and me to be on the same page. All our research was in place but we had to be prepared for the worst. It was important that we discussed the characters we were about to play—the names, backgrounds, families, experiences, qualifications, likes and dislikes, all of it. We decided that Ruhi would pose as a newcomer who had come to Mumbai to try her luck in the film industry. I became the friend who would accompany her to various casting agencies. We fixed the camera in Ruhi's bag and I decided to wear a watch camera as a backup. We decided to meet somewhere close to the office of Saathi Film International the next morning.

Acting Begins

Location: Office of Saathi Film International

Posing as Ruhi Ahmed, who had dreamed of becoming the next Madhuri Dixit, and Bhupen Shah, her companion, we called on the office of Saathi Film International.

We reached at noon, as decided. After going over the details once more, we tried to call the office number listed in the ad but it was temporarily out of service. So we decided to just knock on the door.

We were welcomed by the strong stench of gutkha into a small room that had been divided into two, the walls of which were stained red with the constant spitting. I don't know how Bollywood's *jhakaas* man Anil Kapoor and 'Aakhri Pasta' Chunky Pandey continued to smile in the posters on the walls in that grimy room.

The small space had a wooden table, four plastic chairs for visitors and a wooden shelf with the idols of Hindu gods and goddesses and lit incense sticks. We tried to sit close to the idols, not to pray for a successful sting or our safety, but for some relief from the unbearable odour in the room.

Two men were sitting on revolving chairs, with posters of many struggling actors around them. They were presented to us as big names in the industry, though both of us, as knowledgeable Bollywood buffs, had never seen them. But we played along and admired how they were transforming dreams into reality. I must credit them for their honesty of taking no credit for the career and success of the only two well-known faces on their wall, Anil Kapoor and Chunky Pandey.

However, they did mention that they knew the two very well. Trying to come to the point, Ruhi asked them about the advertisement in the newspaper. Brandishing a broad smile, one of them said, 'Maiiidumb, pahile intra-ducsun to kijiye' (Madam, first introduce yourself).

As per the plan we gave our fake 'intra-ducsun' to the man who identified himself as Mahesh Pancholi and his partner as Salim Sheikh. Since we were lying ourselves, we obviously doubted the credibility of their identities.

They boasted about how the advertisement had got a tremendous response, which was clearly a false claim, especially with a defunct phone. Moreover, there was not a soul except for us. They went on to claim that after auditioning a series of actors, they had almost made up their minds to sign on two actors who they identified as Prashant Navle and Vaishali Patel. They were both experienced artists who had already done a couple of low-budget movies in the past. 'Woh toh dedh lakh rupaya bhi de rahe hain phillam keliye,' (they were even giving Rs 1.5 lakh for the film), boasted Pancholi.

We pretended to be immensely disappointed and almost got up from our seats when he held my hand and said, 'Sad mat hoiye, kuch karte hain. Phillam mein do lead chahiye . . . doosra jodi ab bhi bacha hai' (Don't be sad. We need two leading pairs. The other pair is yet to be cast). But the duo kept emphasizing on the cash that was invested by the first pair again and again, indicating that we would have to buy those roles.

Their reason was that the movie and its success would be a collective responsibility and profit. 'Let us treat this as our project and work together to make it a reality,' were the first words Sheikh said. Pancholi kept saying that he was looking for another fresh pair for the second lead couple and that they would like to cast Ruhi in that second pair. The duo eventually said it in as many words that the other lead pair would have to chip in funds for the project.

Day one had turned out to be quite a surprise for us—exactly the opposite of our anticipations. We had won their confidence in no time. And looking at their body language, I knew they felt positive too. When we were about to ask them a few questions, I saw Sheikh put his hand in his pocket. I thought he was probably pulling out his visiting card but he removed a piece of eight-fold foolscap paper and handed it to me.

While Ruhi and I gazed at each other, not sure of what to do with it, Pancholi said, 'Isscript [script] hai, padh lijiye.' We were stunned to see how casually they handled the script. Hardly a page long, it was a typical tale of two people in love against the wishes of their family and society. The couple fought against all odds, won over their families and lived happily ever, after having achieved their 'Pyaar Ki Aakhiri Manzil'. However, there was no mention of another lead pair, and when we asked them about it, Sheikh told us it was only a rough draft and the script was bound to change.

They were clearly crooks, and I could not help but wonder how they could actually succeed in cheating people. Are struggling actors so vulnerable? I had enough meat for the story, but it had to be brought to a logical end. Ruhi and I took their leave, saying we needed some more time to decide.

The Next Day

Location: Office of Saathi Film International

Excited with the success of the previous day, I arrived earlier than the scheduled meeting time of noon. I didn't go to a coffee shop or restaurant to kill time, but visited a local police station in Sakinaka to meet an officer who had been inviting me for a cup of chai for a very long time.

The officer was my friend from the time I had been an intern with a morning tabloid called the *Daily*. He had saved the day many times when I did not have any story to pitch to editors. He had a great nose for news and had helped me with some big breaks, though he always remained my 'source who requested anonymity'. The secret of his keen eye for news was his hidden desire to be a journalist. Unfortunately for him, his entire village worked in the police and took a lot of pride in the profession, thus leaving no option for him but to continue the legacy.

Considering we were meeting after so long, I dropped the idea of tea and took him for lunch instead. While I rarely discuss unfinished operations, I knew I could trust this man. So I narrated the entire story to him and as usual he provided the kahani mein twist.

He laughed at the mention of Pancholi, Sheikh and their production house. I was sure then that he had some incriminating information against them. And I was right. Growing serious, he said, 'They are cons with multiple cases registered against them. A few months ago, the two were arrested for trafficking a woman and are currently out on bail.' He told me to go ahead with the story and that he would intervene if things got out of hand. Knowing that Pancholi and Sheikh had criminal records made the operation more risky, but I knew this officer was a man of his word and that I could rely on him. I didn't want to worry Ruhi with these details, so I kept them to myself for the time being.

Day Three

Location: Office of Saathi Film International

On reaching their office on the third day, we found that Sheikh was not in and that Pancholi was sitting alone. On inquiring about the former, we learnt that he had gone to meet Vinod and Kavita.

Wondering if they had hired someone else for the project, we expressed our fear at missing out on the part. 'Arey nahi bhai, you are my only stars. I was talking about singers Vinod Rathod and Kavita Krishnamurthy,' he said, naming two of the most successful singers of that era and calling them his childhood buddies. We were pretty sure that he was bluffing.

However, we made him feel as if we were convinced. 'What! Are they going to sing in the film? Thank you Pancholibhai, you have made my friend's life. Aapka yeh ehsaan kaise chukayenge hum?' (How will we repay this debt), I said.

He had an answer ready for that one. With a wide smile, he subtly reminded me that the payment was pending. He gazed at me closely, framing his fingers as though he was looking through a camera and said, 'Shoopper dooper, even you have a face that the camera would love. Why are you shying away, brother? I can cast you opposite your friend.'

This was the first time he had given me a second glance. All this while, he had only spoken to Ruhi. He made it quite obvious that they were more interested in working with female artists than male actors. I was concerned about Ruhi and made sure not to leave her alone in their company.

'Here is the deal. I will give you lead roles in two films provided you chip in Rs 1.5 lakh. These films are definitely going to make you stars overnight, plus the money that we earn out of this project will provide funds for another movie that will land straight in Halliwud.' He meant Hollywood.

Mimicking his smile, I consented. 'Acting ka hunar aapke andar hona chahiye. Uske liye experience ka koi jarurat nahi' (You need talent for acting. Experience is not necessary), he said. Confirming my participation, Pancholi made a call and Sheikh walked in as if he had been waiting at the door for a signal from his partner. Five feet two inches tall and hardly in his twenties, he reminded us that he was our songwriter and lyricist.

'I have written four songs for the movie, all will be super hit,' he claimed.

He opened his book and showed us the songs as proof. 'The script is for a complete two and a half hour love story with four songs and lots of drama,' he said. Pancholi called his office boy Sujit and asked him to give us copies of the script. This time it was typed and had a stamp of Saathi International. In the movie, Raj, a Hindu boy, was supposed to fall in love with Shabnam, a Muslim girl. Both die in the name of love at the end of the two-para script. 'The songs will be the pulse of this movie. There will be outdoor shoots. One song in a park, while the rest at seashores and in market streets,' we were told.

Explaining a song sequence, he said, 'Ruhiji will act upset as you have reached late to meet her in the park. Aap unko rose dete hai, aur woh wahi rose aapke mooh par de mar deti hai' (You give her a rose but she throws it in your face), Pancholi said. Then, as per their plan, we both had to take more than twenty to thirty rounds of a big banyan tree.

Looking at Sheikh, Pancholi said, 'Padho nahi, gaa ke sunao' (Don't read it, sing for them). I was amused by their confidence. Sheikh took the songbook from us and actually started singing one of the tunes. When he started the first line, Pancholi tapped along with his fingers. Ruhi and I somehow managed to control our laughter. The tune was clearly 'inspired' by one of the songs from *Khandaan*, a movie from the 1960s.

By the second *antara* Sheikh was completely engrossed in the music, singing with his eyes shut, despite Pancholi hinting at him to stop. Pancholi even stopped playing the accompanying beat on the table but it hardly affected Sheikh. He had started with the second song when Pancholi raised his voice and said, 'Salim, ruk jaa bhai, baat karni hai' (Salim, stop. We need to talk).

Ruhi interjected at this point with a question. 'When do we have to dance?' 'Gud qoschen' (Good question), Pancholi replied and told us that the entire dance sequence would play out while we were taking rounds of the tree. My head had already started spinning at the mere thought of this dance. I gathered courage and asked if we would have a choreographer to guide us. 'Bhaisahib, it's a low-budget film, we cannot afford a choreographer but we have an in-house talent, Salim. He is a good dancer. He will help us with some steps, and the rest we will have to manage on our own. Shaadi mein dance kiye ho ke nahi . . . haan to bas phir' (Have you danced at weddings? It'll be the same thing).

Pancholi told us that he was waiting for the director, Bachchan Pachera, who was supposed to meet us. 'He is a known artist who is good friends with Ashutosh Gowariker. He has even won a national award for his role of a farmer in *Swades*, which starred Shah Rukh Khan,' he said.

After waiting a little longer, Pancholi asked us to come the next day to meet Pachera. Now this was an interesting twist. They were confidently claiming to know someone who was not as unknown as the rest.

On reaching our office, we did a background check on Bachchan Pachera and found out that he often portrays the role of a poor farmer. He had very small roles in films like *Swades* and a few other Bollywood movies like *Airlift*, *Chillar Party* and *Ragini MMS*. But contrary to what Pancholi had said, he hadn't received any national award. Our film correspondents even got in touch with Gowariker's office, but no one there knew him.

While going through the camera footage we realized we had enough incriminating evidence to nail the cons. Every lie was recorded on the tapes with clear images. However, Pachera had now become an important aspect of this story, and we could not end our story without meeting him.

Final Take/Climax

It was now the fourth day of the sting. We reached their office and found both Pancholi and Sheikh present. After a few minutes of chatting, a handful of men entered the room. They looked to be in their mid to late twenties and surrounded Ruhi and me. It was scary when we realized that they had blocked any chance to escape. I sensed we were in trouble. Maybe they had found out who we were or seen the camera in Ruhi's bag. I dropped the bag on the floor and tried to divert their attention, asking Pancholi whether these men were the junior artists, to which he nodded yes.

I hinted to Ruhi that we should leave but she continued the conversation. Regaining composure, I joined in too and we asked more questions about our director. Sheikh and Pancholi took us to the room inside, claiming that Pachera was secretive about his association with them. After waiting for almost four hours, a man who seemed to be nearing sixty entered the room. He wore jeans and a white T-shirt with sports shoes. As he entered, the atmosphere in the room changed. Sheikh and Pancholi got up, one of them cleaned the table while the other stood behind his chair. Pancholi asked us if we wanted tea and one of the men ran downstairs to get chai for everyone.

After making himself comfortable in one of the revolving chairs, Pachera took out a packet of cigarettes and lit one. Without glancing at us, he took a few more drags and asked Pancholi whether we were the lead pair he was thinking of casting, to which Pancholi nodded in the affirmative. Pachera asked us about our past experience and whether we had acted before. Looking straight into my eyes, he said, 'Dur drishti, kadhi mehnat aur lagan, yeh teen chizein aapko bulandi tak pahuncha sakti hain' (Foresight, hard work and focus will take you to the pinnacle of success).

Pachera boasted about his achievements in the industry and how his role of a poor farmer in *Swades* got him nationwide recognition. He claimed it had got him close to Ashutosh Gowariker and other Bollywood bigwigs. He began dropping names and we nodded along, trying to give him the respect befitting a senior artist in the industry.

We then told Pancholi and the others that we were running out of money and that our family had refused to help us. Pancholi told us again and again that we would miss out on a golden opportunity if the money was not arranged for. As we continued with our helpless tale, Pancholi and Sheikh started bargaining. They then offered us a package deal of ek-pe-ek-free.

The art film for which they had asked Rs 2.5 lakh in the beginning would now be given for free. 'Don't make us bargain more, it is our project and we all have to work together to make this project a reality,' Pancholi said, repeating his favourite line. 'You are the hero and heroine for my next two films and that's final,' he said, sealing the deal and their fates. We had captured the entire conversation on camera but had not yet paid any money. We left their office, promising to return with cash the next day.

Result

We took a day to transcribe the entire conversation and write the story. The next day, we ran a three-page story on the scam, including a piece on the front page of the newspaper. The article received appreciation not only from the police but also from some Bollywood personalities. It was a script better than the one put together by those crooks and the police didn't take long to shut their business down for good. We got many leads from actors who had been betrayed but one particular call left us amused. It was a call from Pancholi.

I smirked when my receptionist told me who was calling. I expected to deal with a couple of fake apologies and regrets. But he said, 'Dekhiye, aapne yeh theek nahin kiya!' I told him that I only exposed the truth and that he had no right to fool innocent aspirants. He continued, 'Haan haan, aap Satyavadi Harishchandra hain, lekin sirf hamare liye kyun? Hum aapko ek secret batate hain. Mere office ke theek bagal mein ek office hai jahan same kaam ho raha hai . . . mera dhandha thapp ho gaya aur woh ab double kama raha hai. Aap uska bhi kuch kijiye na!' (Are you Raja Harishchandra? Why have you done this only to us? After you had us shut down our office, another casting office close to ours is making double the money. Why don't you shut them down too?

I couldn't decide whether to be amazed, amused or shocked by his audacity. With no sense of remorse, he was giving me a lead out of jealousy just to ensure that if he wasn't making money, no one else should either.

Throughout the story I had wondered how such people, who seemed obviously suspect to me, could succeed in duping others. I'm glad that the sting operation helped shut down at least one such business that was taking advantage of innocent people.

TWO

The year 2005 proved to be a turning point in my career. There were many lessons waiting to be learnt. It was the launch year of the much-awaited tabloid *Mumbai Mirror*, and fortunately I was a part of this budding revolution in storytelling and news coverage.

A Times of India Group publication, the tabloid got hold of some of the top journalists in the city who were given a free hand in nailing corrupt babus, uncovering scams, and breaking hard-hitting stories. This freedom was an immense morale booster for journalists like me. It pushed us to work hard as a result of which *Mirror* got several scoops and gave its competitors sleepless nights.

Our bold, fearless and transparent approach built tremendous faith among readers. Many people would wait outside our office to share their stories with us—some personal and many against the system. Whenever the authorities slammed doors in their faces, this aggrieved lot turned to us with expectations. Many times, they had to return disappointed, understanding our limitations. The issues often made us emotional and left us ashamed at the system. At times, it became difficult to convince people that their issues were not addressable. It made them angry. They took revenge by harassing us with incessant calls and humiliating us with baseless allegations.

A Mysterious Encounter

One afternoon, in August 2005, while I was trying hard to find out more details about a case, a man who had been chasing me for over a week to print an article called on my landline number. He was agitated that the cops had not taken action against his neighbour who harassed him. Despite convincing him several times that his case was too petty to merit a First Information Report, he refused to accept it. To vent his anger, he made frantic calls to me to print his story in the newspaper. There were days when he made twenty calls. He even rang up in the middle of the night a couple of times. When he called again that day, I lost my temper. I told him in a harsh tone that I would not take his calls henceforth.

I received another call less than a minute after I had banged the phone down on him. It was the receptionist calling to say that a gentleman was waiting to see me.

I was in no mood to speak to another disgruntled man. I asked the receptionist to take down his contact details and ask him to see me on another day. But this man was adamant. He told the receptionist that he would not leave without seeing me. Somehow, I pushed myself out of my chair to see him. It was one of my best professional decisions yet.

A Vague Lead to a Grave Issue

At the reception, I saw a man sitting on the sofa talking to someone on the phone. Dressed in formal clothes, he sported a big sandalwood tilak and wore thick glasses. He looked confused and scared. As the receptionist guided me to him, we greeted each other with a smile.

Wiping sweat from his forehead, he said, 'I am sorry I cannot tell you who I am. But there is a story brewing in Asia's biggest mental asylum in Thane, the Pradeshik Manorugnalay Regional Mental Hospital. He went on to tell me that many patients admitted to the asylum were actually sane. 'I can help you with only this much information, you will have to investigate the rest.' Saying this, he got up and rushed out of the building as if someone was chasing him.

I wasn't sure whether to take this mysterious man seriously or not. Hoping he wasn't an absconding patient from the asylum, I went back to work. But he had left an impression on my mind and I felt that he could be trusted.

The same day, after work, I discussed the man with our crime editor, S. Hussain Zaidi. Hussain and I had worked together at the city newspaper *Mid-Day* in the past. Fortunately, I got to work under him at *Mumbai Mirror* too. One good thing about working with Hussain was that he gave me complete freedom to pursue stories.

He told me that there could be truth in the man's claim. 'I have heard similar stories from my sources. It is worth your time. I am trying to trace a patient who has been in the asylum for the last twenty years,' he said. I was now sure that it was a lead worth following.

Research and Recce

To begin with, I researched how patients could be admitted to the asylum. According to the Mental Health

Act, 1987, there are two ways. The patient can either be admitted following magisterial orders or voluntarily, in which case a patient is known as a voluntary boarder. In normal circumstances, if the patient is an adult then his or her consent must be taken before admission. However, in special circumstances, which means a circumstance where the mentally ill person does not, or is unable to, express willingness for admission as a voluntary patient, he or she may be admitted on an application made by a relative or a friend.

Every application should be submitted with medical certificates from two medical practitioners stating that the person is medically unfit. In case there are no such certificates, the medical officer in-charge of the asylum can admit the patient after certification from two medical practitioners working in the asylum's hospital or nursing home.

With such lengthy and clear guidelines in place, it was impossible to imagine that illegal activities were taking place. But a visit to the hospital changed my mind.

The Asylum

Spread across more than an acre, the compound had a lot of greenery. You could hear patients in different languages screaming, singing, reciting poems and offering prayers.

Most of the patients were lodged in two- or three-storeyed stone buildings that had a remarkable resemblance to Indian jails. Only the mentally stable patients could venture into the garden for a stroll. As you passed by the buildings, you could see some patients standing at the gates and staring at one spot without blinking.

When I had spoken to some of the staff on the phone earlier, they had told me that there were around 500 patients who had been abandoned by their families for various reasons. The asylum then had a capacity of around 1350 patients but accommodated 1800 patients at any given point of time.

Three-level Hurdle

After taking a stroll around the hospital, I went to the office, wanting to know the procedure for voluntary admission. I was told there were three stages to getting a person admitted.

First, I would have to meet the doctor in the OPD and convince him or her about admitting the patient. Then the doctor would examine the patient and, if things went smoothly, prepare the medical papers.

At the next stage, I would have to meet a social worker from the psychiatric department with the papers, who would cross-check my credentials and interview the patient at length. The staff at the hospital told me that the social worker usually interrogated patients about their background and medical history before referring the patient to the last and final authority, the superintendent of the asylum.

The next morning, I discussed the challenges with Hussain. After almost an hour-long discussion on the pros and cons, we thought of roping in two female staffers for the story. One would pose as my wife and the second would be my sister. I would pretend to be a middle-class working man who wanted to have his wife admitted to the asylum.

For the role of my wife, we chose one of my closest friends and colleagues, Rimona Ellis. My usual partner in crime, Naveeta Singh, would pretend to be my sister. Rimona, a fresh journalism graduate, had been working with the team for less than a year while Naveeta and I had worked together at *Mid-Day*.

It was decided that Rimona wouldn't talk much and in case the doctors asked her many questions, she would just answer, 'Mi bari aahe' (I am okay in Marathi) or 'theek hun'. I knew this was a dialogue the asylum staff heard from patients when they were brought to the hospital.

Naveeta was there to bail me out if I fumbled or got stuck answering questions. Her backstory was that she was Smita, married and living with her husband outside Mumbai. We went over the story again and again for a day, doing our best to make it sound real. Rimona decided to stick to her first name.

Day One

Since I had visited the hospital the day before, I went straight to the front office desk and asked the staff about the admission procedure. I spoke to a peon, who was a middle-aged Marathi-speaking man. He turned out to be very helpful and gave me detailed information. During his long explanation, he asked, 'Who is the patient?'

To cut him off, I jokingly said, 'Mi aahe' (It's me). On hearing this, he backed away from me. Watching me smile, he said, 'Kya saab, aap bhi majjak kartai' (Sir, you are pulling my leg). But this did not stem his lengthy monologue. He went on about the procedure. Finally, I excused myself on the pretext of making a phone call. After some time, I went back to him, thinking he would change the topic. He started with another set of questions. Fed up, I coughed and made to move away. This time he realized I was trying to end the conversation. Miffed, he asked me to see the peon to the hospital's superintendent.

On my visit I realized that the peon lobby is more powerful than the officials at the asylum. They ran a parallel administration network by mediating for the doctors at the hospital. I was not surprised, since this is the case in every government office.

I slipped a Rs 100 note into the pocket of the peon to the hospital's superintendent, asking for the inside details. Without further ado, he directed me to another peon, claiming he had answers to all my queries. This man, according to the superintendent's peon, was key to all the activities of the hospital, as he was the superintendent's most trusted associate. When I found this associate, he told me I could not meet the doctor that day as he was busy. I decided to pack up for the day.

Day Two

The next day, the peons and the patients greeted me with smiles. After just one visit of a few hours, I had become a familiar face in the hospital.

Slightly nervous, I entered the waiting area outside the superintendent's office. I saw several patients and their relatives waiting in the corridor to meet him. I spoke to some of them. Many wanted their relatives who were admitted to the hospital to stay there longer. I saw an old man dressed in a white kurta and dhoti, standing in the corner of the lobby with a well-built man, who I later found out was his son. The old man had tied his son's hands behind his back with a nylon rope. The son was walking up and down the lobby but it did little to calm him.

The old man told me he was his only son and that he had lost all hope that he would ever get better. 'I just want him to stay here so that I can be at peace in my home town in Pune. I have tried all the remedies and met almost all the psychiatrists in Mumbai and Pune, but my son has not shown any sign of improvement. At my age, I cannot chase him all the time. If he stays here I can focus on my farming and earn money to pay for his fees in the asylum,' he said.

He looked hopeful that the doctor would bail him out of the situation. I saw a peon coming out of the superintendent's office and rushed to him. He scanned me from head to toe and asked, 'What do you want?'

I told him that I wanted to meet the doctor to admit my wife who was mentally unstable. The peon gave me another suspicious look. He assessed every person carefully before they met his boss.

He took me outside the office and asked me to meet one of the other peons to know the exact procedure. Instead, I went down the stairs. He followed me to the gate. Knowing he was keeping a close watch on me, I changed direction and pretended to talk on the phone. I had gauged that the superintendent's peon was key to this operation and if I won his confidence, half my work would be done.

He watched me for a while from a distance but since he was carrying some files for the doctor's reference, he left soon. I was dejected, thinking I had raised his suspicions. I gathered courage and went back to him. He greeted me with a smile. I told him again that I needed to see the superintendent since I wished to admit my wife who needed psychiatric treatment.

He kept looking at me suspiciously. Peons are usually extremely cautious. Before arranging meetings with doctors, they ensure that there are no cameras or recording equipment hidden in visitors' clothes. To gain the peon's confidence, I removed my jacket and tried to reassure him. I was right about what had been bothering him, because he said, 'You cannot come wearing such jackets to meet the sahib. It could arouse unnecessary suspicion and your work will get stuck.'

I looked confidently into his eyes. After a while he said, 'You can meet him tomorrow.' Thankfully, his scanning eyes had missed the camera behind one of my shirt buttons.

While I was trying to calm my racing heart, his eyes paused on something on my shirt. Pointing towards my pocket he asked, 'What is this?' I froze. He reached forward and removed the pen I was carrying, examining it.

'It's just a pen. Keep it, brother. I got it from my office. You don't have to return it,' I said, even though it was one of my treasured Parkers. Shamelessly, he kept it. 'Come tomorrow and I will arrange your meeting with sahib,' he said.

It is hard to trust someone these days, the peon said, adding that he would help me since I was a Marathi *manoos* (a Maharashtrian). He informed me that the doctor was available only two days in a week. He took down my number and assured me that he would get me for an appointment, saying, 'Don't worry, *bhau*.' I was more confident this time. I could see that he had regained his faith because apart from the Parker, I had also slyly given him Rs 500.

On reaching office, I told everyone about my day, and after a lot of discussion it was decided that it would be risky to carry the camera on me.

With the help of our technicians, we analysed all the options and finally decided that Naveeta would be ideal to handle the camera. Since it was not feasible to fix the camera on her clothes, as the set-up required frequent change of batteries, we decided to fix it to her purse. Makeup artists were called to make Rimona look like a Maharashtrian housewife. They made her wear a sari, green bangles and a big bindi.

As Naveeta had not handled a camera in the past, she was given basic instructions on operating it.

Day Three

We were nervous as we reached the hospital.

As soon as we entered the premises, one of the patients who had been allowed into the garden for a stroll began chasing Rimona.

Thinking that he might attack, Naveeta and Rimona started walking faster. The man tried to match their steps. All my efforts to calm them down did not help. 'Girls, he will copy your actions, so just stop,' I said. They did and then so did the man.

'Give me some money, *tai*' (elder sister in Marathi), the man said. The more we tried to avoid him, the more he chased us. Though he sounded sober, the chase had got scary by now. Thankfully, a warden came looking for him and he was escorted back to his ward.

It was time to begin the operation. We went straight to the OPD section where we met a doctor who conducted preliminary investigations. 'Sir, I am Deepak Sonawane. I work as a software engineer and this is my wife, Rimona, and my sister, Smita,' I said. From the first meeting itself, we felt that this doctor was a sincere guy. He never demanded any money and asked us many questions. One of the questions that we were unprepared for was how we had met.

Thankfully, I remembered an article my colleague had written about a love story gone sour. I replaced its cast and used it as my own. I told the doctor that I had met Rimona in an online chatroom. Over time, we started liking each other and decided to marry in April 2003. Just a year after the marriage, her behaviour changed. I told him she would suddenly become violent and attack people.

Hearing this, the doctor tried to move away from Rimona, who was sitting close to him. 'All this while I was thinking that this one (pointing towards Naveeta sitting on the other side of the table) is the patient. You should take precaution while getting patients to the hospital,' he said. He continued to ask us questions, which went on for nearly an hour. Finally, he prepared the medical papers and asked us to see a social worker. The doctor mentioned in the paper that the family wanted to admit the patient.

The second round of questioning by the social worker went off smoothly. She made basic queries about residence proof and Rimona's medical history.

I told her that since I stayed on the ground floor of the building, all the medical papers and residence proof had been destroyed in the flooding on 26 July that year. I had been caught off guard by this question. This too was from an article I had read. Without any further questions, she referred me to the superintendent.

This was my second attempt to meet him and I was confident it would work out. Seeing the long queue outside his office, Naveeta hinted to me that she needed to switch off the camera to conserve the batteries for the right moment. She left on the pretext of going to the washroom and I accompanied her to show her the way, leaving Rimona in the queue.

Suddenly, I heard a loud scream. I recognized Rimona's voice. I was surprised as this was not planned.

I thought she was overacting but then I saw something that frightened me too. A tall hefty man was standing in front of Rimona. She had not noticed him all this while since she had been too engrossed in staring at the floor quietly.

On seeing the commotion, the superintendent's peon rushed over. Her scream worked in our favour as he was convinced she had a tendency to get violent. He put us in the front of the queue to meet the doctor. 'Good going, girl,' I whispered into Rimona's ear. 'The scream was real,' she replied.

In just a few minutes, we were called to see the doctor. Unfortunately, Naveeta had not returned with her camera from the washroom. To buy time I entered his cabin first and asked Rimona to wait outside. I had never seen the doctor before.

I saw two men behind the desk. I assumed the man sitting in the main chair was the superintendent, who gestured for me to take a seat. He kept addressing the other man as 'Doctor' and kept talking to him about a common patient. I gathered that the man sitting next to the superintendent was a renowned psychiatrist in Mumbai. Interrupting the conversation, the superintendent turned towards me and asked, 'Yes, what do you want?' I repeated the story about how I wanted to admit my wife to the hospital for treatment. He asked me about the medical papers and other documents required for admission, and I told him that the documents had been lost in the 26 July floods. He looked at the other doctor, who was also not convinced. They looked at me, amused. I felt dejected. This meeting was jinxed. Even the camera was not in place.

Suddenly, the other doctor looked at his watch and realized that he had to leave. He got up and said, 'I should take your leave, doctor, I have an important appointment.'

As soon as he left, I saw Naveeta and Rimona enter the office. I introduced them to the doctor and looked at Naveeta to ask if the camera was rolling. She nodded subtly.

I noticed a change in the superintendent's tone, as if he had been waiting for the other doctor to leave the office. 'How will I admit her? You don't even have her papers,' he said with a smile. To support my story, Naveeta talked about how difficult it had become for me to focus on work and home. She told him that she had to leave her husband's home and stay with me to take care of Rimona.

The doctor interrupted, 'Where do you stay?' Both Naveeta and I replied at the same time, but gave different answers. I said Ahmed Nagar and Naveeta replied Pune. We both looked at each other nervously. The doctor realized that something was amiss.

I didn't want to give him a chance to think about it further, so I quickly clarified that she had a house in Ahmed Nagar and Pune. Her husband stayed in Ahmed Nagar as his office was close by, but Naveeta lived with her children in Pune and kept shuttling between the two cities. The doctor was still not convinced. 'How can I trust you when there are so many gaps in your story?' he asked. He then asked us to meet his peon. The peon told us that we would have to pay Rs 5000 for the admission. 'Is that the fees?' Naveeta asked. 'No, it is not. You will not be given any receipts for the payment. You come with the amount tomorrow and your work will be done,' the peon replied.

Before we left the hospital, the peon took us to the man who had directed us to the superintendent in the first place. He seemed to handle all the dirty work for the corrupt doctor. He had been with the doctor for several years and was one of his most trusted accomplices. We were told he would talk to us on behalf of the doctor and that we should coordinate with him for the procedure.

In the middle of the conversation, he removed a tiny brass box from his pocket that had tobacco. Mixing the tobacco on his palm, he said, 'Don't worry, I know your case very well. Your work is done. You keep your commitments and we will do the rest for you.' He asked us to see him the next day.

On reaching office we went through the footage to ascertain whether we had enough evidence to nail the doctor. We had caught all the exchanges on camera. We just needed one final take.

Days Four and Five

The next two days were slow as I visited the hospital to inquire whether we could get Rimona admitted. On these days, the man whom we were supposed to coordinate with could not reach the hospital since there was a major issue with the local trains. On the fifth day, I got a chance to meet the superintendent for the second time. He asked me to come with the patient the next day for admission. He even told me to talk to the peon before leaving the hospital.

Day Six: The Final Take

I felt like it was the first day of my board exams. If anything went wrong, all our efforts would go waste. I cracked stupid jokes on our way to the hospital to try and lighten the mood, but Rimona and Naveeta knew that I was as nervous as them.

There were a dozen ways it could all go wrong. What if Rimona was admitted? How would we get her out? What if we could not rescue her? We were all thinking about this but none of us voiced these concerns.

We headed straight to the superintendent's office without realizing that we had not switched on the camera. On seeing us, the man who would take the money asked us to wait outside. Naveeta made an excuse to go to the washroom, saying Rimona had to use it urgently, so that she could switch on the camera.

The doctor's associate seemed more cautious today. I saw him looking at us several times. I was worried that if he passed by the ladies' toilet, which was on the ground floor of the same building, he would be suspicious if he knew Naveeta was inside the washroom instead of Rimona. To keep him where I could see him, I kept conversing with him about his absence the other day. The easiest way to connect with people in Mumbai, especially Maharashtrians, is to inquire about their home town and village. When I brought up the topic, he went on and on about his village and relatives. I wasn't really paying attention to the conversation as I was thinking about the camera.

Finally, I saw Naveeta and Rimona approaching us and I calmed down. There were not many patients in the lobby that day but the superintendent seemed to be busy with some administrative work due to which we had to wait for almost half an hour. Considering the battery life of the camera was only one hour, Naveeta excused herself again on the pretext of going to the washroom. The associate asked her to come fast as 'sahib' could call at any moment. We couldn't decide whether to keep the camera on hold for some more time or to switch it off. When Naveeta was heading to the washroom, I messaged her, suggesting that she should switch it off to conserve the battery. In case the superintendent called us in, I would enter his office first and they should quickly leave for the washroom to switch it on again.

At last, after waiting for almost four hours, the superintendent rang the bell outside his office to call his man in, who came out to inform us that the doctor would now see us. Naveeta said she would follow later. Without further queries, his associate added, 'Go madam, but come fast, the doctor won't wait for too long.'

As soon as I entered his cabin, I pretended to make a call on my phone. I told the doctor my mother was on the line and I needed to talk to her urgently. I carried on a false conversation till Naveeta and Rimona entered the cabin. Without wasting a second, he asked us to fill up a form and return to him once we were done. We gave a fake address and no one asked for any proof. On all the papers we mentioned only our cell phone numbers, but no one cross-checked even once to see if they were authentic.

After filling the forms, we went to see the superintendent again. He went through the form and finally gave the green signal for the admission by signing on it. All this while, the camera was rolling and the entire conversation was captured uninterrupted. The superintendent referred us to the women's ward so that Rimona could be admitted. As we came out of the superintendent's cabin, we knew we had cracked the story of the year.

The Impact

The story was appreciated across media channels. They all reached the hospital the day after our article was published. There were reactions from various government departments seeking action against the hospital authorities. Woken up by the *Mumbai Mirror* exposé, the state government set up a five-member committee to investigate the matter. Former director of health services Dr Subhash Salunkhe sent a senior-level officer to investigate the matter. The committee was asked to submit its report in three days.

On the day the story was published we received several calls on our office number from people who had similar complaints against the superintendent. They called with details of how he had a rate card for all his dirty deals. The doctor didn't just charge for admission, but also asked for Rs 20,000–25,000 for a mental illness certificate.

The Stunned Caller

One caller particularly asked to speak to me. 'You are a terrific actor,' the voice said.

'I am sorry, who is this?' I asked. He identified himself as the senior doctor who had been in the office talking to the superintendent.

'What a surprise, doctor. How have you been?' I said.

'Hats off to you guys. I am stunned by the fact that you were an undercover reporter. Superb work, keep it up,' he said before hanging up.

The Superintendent Suspended

Based on the report submitted by the inquiry committee, former state health minister Vimal Mundada suspended the superintendent. Taking lessons from our report and due to the mounting pressure, the minister even deputed women counsellors in an effort to ensure that the asylum would not be used by people wanting to get rid of unwanted female relations.

Calling the superintendent's conduct unethical and immoral, the minister said that asylum officials in Thane had done a disservice to their profession by admitting a perfectly normal and sane individual. A simultaneous inquiry was also initiated against the doctor by the Anti-Corruption Bureau of Maharashtra. All the 200 patients admitted by the superintendent were put under the scanner. He was suspended for several months.

But like every government inquiry this never saw the light of day. Despite all the assurances to take the strictest action against the doctor, the inquiry committee has done a shoddy job. Eventually the doctor was reinstated in some hospital outside the state, but he was never posted in Thane again.

When I had begun the sting I hadn't expected to find such a complex network of people so dedicated to pulling off a scam. What came across in each interaction was that they had absolutely no qualms about treating patients unfairly, not only exposing them to mistreatment but also facilitating others to maliciously have relatives admitted. It exposed the ugly side of an institution that is entrusted with keeping the more vulnerable members of our society from harming themselves and others. Though our operation was planned in detail, we could easily have been caught or our admission could have been rejected if only the authorities had been strict about actually examining the patient and accepting legal documents.

THREE

There was chaos everywhere. People were screaming, some clutching at their wounds, while more lay lifeless on the ground. At first, no one could tell the site of the blast, but as police arrived at the Gateway of India, it slowly became apparent that the blackened husk of a car was where the bomb had gone off. While the cops gathered evidence and surveyed the scene, news trickled in that another bomb had gone off in Zaveri Bazaar.

* * *

Around Lunchtime

Mid-Day office

25 August 2003

'Vineet, you are an amazing guy and a very dear friend. But that's about it. I have never thought of you as anything more. Sorry, I am already seeing someone.'

'Who the hell sent this mail to Ankita?' my colleague Vineet Vallikapan yelled as he read an email in his inbox in the newsroom. Vineet and Ankita were the talk of the newsroom despite being 'just friends' because of the way he used to flirt with her.

He scanned his mailbox frantically. To his horror, he discovered a mail sent to Ankita that read, 'Hi Ankita, I have been holding this confession back for a while now but cannot continue doing so any longer. I think I have developed feelings beyond just friendship for you and I cannot hide it any more. Please come to office in a red dress tomorrow if you have the same feelings for me. No matter what your answer is, we shall always remain good friends.'

His reaction had caught everyone's attention. Now the entire newsroom was waiting for Ankita to return from the washroom. As she walked back towards her desk, she couldn't help but blush looking at Vineet. 'That wasn't me, Ankita,' Vineet said. She replied, 'You don't have to clarify, I have mailed you my answer.'

'What do I do?' Vineet said looking at me while I tried hard to control my laughter. Everyone was amused by what had happened. 'You wear red almost every day, Ankita. I was wondering why you wore green today!' said our city editor Lajwanti D'Souza.

Unique like her name, Lajwanti has been one of the best team leaders I have worked with. I owe some of my best memories of journalism to her. We felt like a college group rather than a news team. She would ensure we stayed in high spirits, even on tough assignments. There was never a dull moment with her. Just as we were about to get back to work, her phone rang. 'What!' she exclaimed after answering her phone. 'Who are you and where are you calling from?' The person on the other end had already cut the call by then though.

Without wasting a second, Lajwanti immediately switched to work mode and said, 'Guys, there seems to have been a blast at the Gateway of India. Get confirmations now.'

The smiles vanished from everyone's faces and we started tapping our sources to confirm the news. Some reporters called the police control room, while others contacted the civil hospitals and the fire brigade. It didn't take long for the news to be confirmed as the phones started ringing endlessly. People called to tell us what they had seen and to inform us about casualties.

After a series of calls, the preliminary information suggested that there had been two blasts in the city during the lunch hour. One in a taxi parked near the Gateway of India and the other at Zaveri Bazaar, the city's prominent jewellery market. The blasts claimed fifty-two innocent lives while more than 250 people had been injured. After a brief chat, a team of reporters was sent to different spots with photographers. I was asked to stay in office and get details on the police investigation. I had never imagined in my wildest dreams that this would take me to Dubai.

From the day of the blast till the arrest of the conspirators, I closely followed each and every development in the case. The Crime Branch officials cracked the case and arrested Mohammad Hanif Abdul Rahim Sayyed and his wife along with their associates in September 2003. Following a tip that the key conspirator of the twin blasts, Hanif, had been indoctrinated by a mastermind in Dubai, it seemed best for me to make a quick visit to the place where all of it had allegedly been plotted.

* * *

It was a hot and sunny afternoon on 14 September 2003, my third day in Dubai. I was on my way to the Jumeirah beach, one of the most popular tourist destinations in the city. As I strolled leisurely, I saw the blue-paned Hilton Dubai Jumeirah hotel standing tall against the backdrop of the clear blue sky. I took a few pictures of the building and then looked for a bus stand, so that I could get back to my hotel in Deira. As I was walking to the bus stand, a purple car came to a screeching halt near me. Two men dressed in loose ankle-length dishdashas got out, flashed their ID cards that had a logo that resembled the CID emblem, and asked me to raise my hands. One of them frisked me to check if I was carrying any weapons. The two emptied my bag on the bonnet of their car and examined every item in the bag. They must have been disappointed, as they did not find anything except a harmless camera.

They ordered me to get into the car without giving me any explanation. Sitting in the back seat, I could hear them talking in Arabic but I had no sense of what they were saying. One of them asked me why I was visiting Dubai and where I lived in India. I told them I lived in Mumbai and tried to get them to talk by asking if they had ever visited my home town. One of the officers said he had never been to the city because it had been witness to many bomb blasts. After driving for a few kilometres, the car slowed and then stopped on the side of the road. The duo informed me that they were waiting for their friend. My anxiety increased with every passing minute. Despite having seen their ID cards I wondered if they were real cops.

My doubts were put to rest when I saw a white police van approaching us. I was handed over to two policemen who were not as gentle as the earlier ones and pushed me into the van. I had no idea where I was being taken. As we drove, I could see the names of prominent shopping centres and hotels on my way to an unknown destination.

After about five kilometres, the van took a turn after a signboard indicating the route to the Dubai police headquarters. I was pulled out of the van and pushed into a room of about 300 square feet already occupied by about seventeen inmates.

Before allowing me to take a seat in the crowded room, the cops who had brought me to the headquarters took away all my belongings, including my camera, without telling me what crime I had committed. After pushing me into the room, the cop who had accompanied me handed me over to another police officer who was manning the crowd in the lockup. I was asked to take a seat between two hefty men who constantly stared at me.

Afraid of getting bashed up on my first day in custody, I sat quietly. After an awkward silence, I tried to strike up a conversation with one of them. The man sitting next to me turned out to be a Pakistani national. 'I was brought here fifteen days ago, no one has bothered to tell me the reason till date. My passport and other documents have been confiscated,' he said. His words made me numb. I thought that the cops had figured out I was really in Dubai to find out more about Hanif, and that I would not be let off any time soon. But who had spilled the beans? Was it the manager of the Hilton from whom I had sought information on the Mumbai blast conspirator or the electrician in the back office? I thought back, trying to figure out how I had ended up behind bars in an unknown country, among unknown people and with no way to contact anyone.

Flashback

Hilton Dubai Jumeirah

Just before the arrest.

During Hanif's interrogations, the Crime Branch had found out that he worked as an electrician at the Hilton till he was asked to shave off his beard. The other reason he left was that he had to deal with alcohol and women, which he considered to be against his religion. Thinking that I would find out more about this brainwashed man, I visited the hotel, posing as his friend. When I asked the staff about Hanif, they behaved weirdly. Some feigned ignorance while others asked me to leave the premises for fear of having the police turn up at their doorsteps.

At the reception, I saw a tall man who looked like he might be Pakistani. He wore a dark blue blazer and was busy answering calls from hotel rooms. When he paused in between calls, I quickly approached him. 'Where can I meet Hanif?' I asked.

He pointed towards the back office, where the electrical engineering department was. I had thought I would be thrown out of the hotel in seconds, but the reaction was the exact opposite. The man had not even bothered to give me a second look.

In the electrical department, a man was sitting on a chair, trying to repair a device with a screwdriver. He seemed engrossed in his work and I went unnoticed for several seconds despite standing close to him. Finally I spoke up. 'I am here to see Hanif.' His expression changed instantly.

The man, whose name I found out was Ramon, opened his eyes wide and said, 'How do you know Hanif?

You don't know where he is? Don't ask about him, you will be in trouble,' he warned.

When I pressed him for more information, Ramon added, 'He was working here for a time but has left the job. Since his arrest, lots of CID officials visit the hotel premises in civil clothes. Go away before you get into any trouble.'

At the Hilton, Hanif was paid a monthly salary of 1700 dirhams (around Rs 20,400). He used to stay with other employees in the staff quarters of the hotel. He started out in Dubai at the Saudi Oger construction company, which had its office in Emirates Tower. He then quit in September 1999, after being offered a better job at the Hilton.

Ramon went back to his work and pretended to be busy. I stood there thinking he might restart the conversation and reveal more information about his colleague who was currently in the custody of Mumbai Police. But he ignored me. When I continued standing, he said in a firm voice, 'Please leave.' I had no choice.

These were the only two people with whom I had interacted at the hotel before the cops came looking for me. I suspected the man at the front desk more since he had refused to make eye contact with me. Also, before I left the hotel, I saw this man talking on the phone to someone. I had hardly suspected him then but after my run-in with the police, I was quite convinced he was the one who had reported me. One thing was clear from the behaviour of these two men: everyone was afraid to talk about Hanif. Police investigations revealed that, during his stay in Dubai, Hanif offered namaz five to six times a day in a mosque close to his workplace. One of the regular visitors was a person who was part of a fundamentalist group and was charged with recruiting people like Hanif to execute terror activities in India. Once indoctrinated, Hanif returned to India and began working as an auto driver in Mumbai. He stayed with his family in Chimatpada chawl in Andheri.

During his stay in Mumbai, Hanif founded a group named Gujarat Revenge Force, whose motive was to avenge the Godhra riots. Abdul Rehman Aydeed alias Nasir was Hanif's associate and a resident of Crawford Market in Mumbai. A college dropout, Nasir went to Dubai in 1996. He worked as a clerk in the Dubai municipality for some time. During his stay in Dubai, he was roped in by one of the ISI-sponsored terrorist outfits, Lashkar-e-Taiba. He was indoctrinated and trained in the use of firearms and explosives. Nasir, who was killed in an encounter with Mumbai Police just a few days after the arrest of Hanif and his wife, helped the group with the logistics required to make the bomb and place it, while his wife Fahmida Sayyed acted as an adviser.

Given his experience as an electrician, Hanif had also been trained to assemble a bomb using gelatine sticks and batteries. He collaborated with a man called Ashrat Shafiq Ansari, an embroidery worker who lived in Juhu galli. Ashrat had first-hand experience of the Godhra violence and had fled from Surat after hearing of a rampaging mob headed towards his city from Ahmedabad.

The Gujarat Revenge Force chose only Gujarati populated areas to send a clear message about their motive. They have been charged with two more terror attacks—a bomb blast in a bus at Ghatkopar on 28 July 2003; and an unexploded bomb at the Seepz Bus Depot planted on 2 December 2002.

The year 2003 was considered to be the rebirth of terrorism in Mumbai. The Crime Branch and Mumbai Police did not usually have to cope with such attacks and pressure. Unlike the underworld, they had no network in the terror field. That's why, despite their claims of having arrested those involved in the bomb blasts, the explosions continued and people kept dying. With a limited taskforce, Hanif managed to elude the investigating agencies for almost two months, from the time of the Ghatkopar blast in July 2003 till his arrest in the last week of August.

The Mistake that Led to Hanif's Arrest

The first clue in the case came when one of the key witnesses, the owner of the taxi that exploded at the Gateway of India, walked into the police station and provided details of the blast.

Shivnarayan Pandey told the police that Hanif, his wife Fahmida and two daughters travelled in his cab for two days; he was hired for Rs 1000 to tour the city. Meanwhile, Ashrat Shafiq Ansari, Hanif's associate hired another taxi. The bombs were placed in the boots and were timed to explode at 1 p.m. on 25 August 2003. Ashrat went straight to Zaveri Bazaar. Hanif, Fahmida and their two daughters, sixteen-year-old Farheen and four-year-old Shakira, sat in Pandey's vehicle and headed to the Gateway of India.

At Zaveri Bazaar, Ashrat pretended to wait for someone. After some time, he asked the driver to park the cab and wait as he wanted to buy some material. He got out and began walking towards Charni Road station, the closest railway station. He had barely walked 200 metres when he heard an explosion. It was 12.40 p.m.

Meanwhile at the Gateway of India, Hanif asked Pandey to park in a pay-and-park enclosure near the seaside parapet just across the Taj Mahal Hotel. While Hanif was hurrying away from the taxi, Pandey asked him, 'Sahib, time lagega kya' (Will you take time)? Hanif nodded and left the spot.

He regretted this reply later, said an officer who was close to the investigations. Before leaving their homes that day, the group had decided that they would ensure that the taxi drivers would remain in the cab so that they would be killed in the blasts. 'If I would have assured the taxi driver I would return in a short while he would have stayed back in his vehicle and died in the blast. It was the biggest mistake of my life,' Hanif told a Crime Branch officer during interrogation.

Pandey proved to be a vital witness in the breakthrough of the case. He gave the minutest details of the family and also informed the authorities of the particular spot in Andheri where Hanif had boarded his taxi. With the help of sketches made by the artists based on descriptions provided by Pandey, the cops scanned the area. Finally, they found a man who had seen Hanif and his family boarding the cab from the said spot. He was in love with Hanif's older daughter Farheen and had been following her regularly. That's how he was able to provide accurate details about the family.

A few days after the blast, when the police knocked on Hanif's door, no one was at home. Soon, a special team dressed as vegetable vendors, hawkers and beggars laid a trap. Every person entering the area was monitored. The cops feared that the family might have fled from their home as news of the taxi driver's inputs had already reached the media. After waiting for almost an entire day, the family returned to their home and was picked up by the Crime Branch. The officer could hardly believe that they had cracked the case.

Many dark aspects of Mumbai's history have been associated with Dubai in one way or another. In the second week of September 2003, a close friend and a popular cop told me about a mosque in Dubai where young people were brainwashed. He told me that Hanif had only been a foot soldier, and that the mastermind was somewhere in Dubai, indoctrinating the youngsters to join the jihad.

After talking to more officers who were closely involved in the investigations, I decided that the tip was worth taking a risk on. I discussed the idea in office and everyone saw its potential.

But not all stings go as planned. You pull some off while others are abruptly and drastically cut short by extenuating circumstances. Even though I had known

The Anatomy of a Sting

that there was a significant amount of danger and a high chance of not unearthing much evidence, I had never expected that I would be arrested so soon after arriving in Dubai. The reactions of the staff at the hotel had shown me just how scared they were of talking about Hanif and that there was clearly more to the matter than met the eye.

* * *

It was almost afternoon by now. Despite my repeated requests none of the officers agreed to help me make a call to arrange for some help.

The prisoners who had finished their lunch wanted to nap but didn't have enough space. Those who were brought after me argued with the on-duty cop, clueless as to why they had been arrested.

Suddenly an official arrived and announced the names of some of the prisoners from a list in his hand. He called out my name too, leaving me anxious about what lay ahead.

We were asked to stand in a queue outside the cell. Once all the inmates had gathered, they asked us to move towards the lobby. Each of us was given a slate that had our name and other details, such as age, nationality and purpose of visit mentioned on it. One by one we were pushed in front of a photographer who took our pictures, including profile shots.

We were then directed to the fingerprint bureau of the unit and were asked to give our prints on a sheet of paper for the record. I almost felt like a criminal for a crime I was unaware of. The mental trauma was getting more unbearable with every passing hour.

The moment I consoled myself that everything would be all right, I was put through some form of humiliation. While I was waiting in line for the fingerprints, I excused myself on the pretext of going to the washroom, just a few steps away. To my surprise, the officer allowed us to take a loo break without an escort.

As I entered the washroom, I saw one of the other guys taking out a cell phone from his undergarment. He made a call to one of his relatives to inform them about his arrest.

From his conversation, I realized that this man was a Pakistani. He turned out to be a messiah. When I asked him if I could make a call, he offered me his phone without any hesitation and my heart went out to him. Luckily, I remembered the phone number of one of my friends and messaged him about my arrest, not knowing whether he would receive it.

We were brought back to our cell after the photos and fingerprints had been taken. The jail was almost full, with over five to six hundred inmates. They all had the same question—what had brought them there—and the same hope of being rescued. Some said that it was just a routine round-up while others claimed that the operation was a precautionary action in the wake of an international conference that the UAE was about to host in the coming week.

As the clock struck seven, all the staff sitting began winding up, indicating the end of their duty. The new set of officers seemed to be more aggressive than the previous lot. They demanded strict discipline among inmates and ensured pin-drop silence in the cell. Talking had been the only way of passing the time, but now that was forbidden.

I waited for dinnertime, not because I was hungry but so that I may have another opportunity to access the phone. But all my hopes were shattered when two men came from the canteen with dinner.

The prisoners were served rice and fish with gravy. On any other day at home I would have enjoyed the food, but the mental agony had taken a toll on my appetite. Every minute seemed like an hour. I was certain that this place would be home indefinitely. With no sign of help so far, it seemed that the message sent to my friend had not been delivered. I had even sent my friend the number of my bosses and colleagues so that he could make a few calls and seek help.

Around 10 p.m., I saw a senior officer entering the cell. As soon as he entered the room, the junior staff got up from their seats. He looked around, asked the officers a few questions and left. The officer attending to the prisoners looked at me and asked me to follow him to an adjacent room, where the senior officer was waiting for me. He took my belongings out of a bag, keeping them in front of his superior. Of all the belongings, he lifted the camera and asked, 'What's in this?'

I feared that if I told him the purpose of my visit to Dubai, they would keep me in jail longer. I gathered courage and maintained that I had come for a tour, saying that I was clicking pictures at Jumeirah beach when the cops caught me. I told him that the camera had a few photographs that I had clicked just minutes before the cops arrested me.

'Are you telling the truth?' the officer asked me, to which I firmly replied, 'You can develop the films and verify.' He had a short conversation with his junior in Arabic. 'You can go,' he finally said.

Not realizing that my release would take place so abruptly, I asked him once again, 'What, sir? What did you just say?'

'You may leave,' he repeated. Without thinking further, I collected all my belongings and stuffed them in my backpack. My steps faltered as I nearly ran out of the headquarters, unable to believe my luck. After almost half a kilometre, I slowed down and saw a cab waiting by the side of the road. I opened the door and sat inside it without saying a word to the driver.

Considering how strict the Dubai police was, I knew I had been lucky to be let off. So I decided to drop the case and return home. I still wonder what I would have found out if only I had been able to dig further. In February 2012 the high court confirmed the death sentence to Ashrat Shafiq Ansari (34), Mohammad Hanif Abdul Rahim Sayyed (46) and his wife Fahmida Sayyed (43) for claiming the lives of fifty-two persons and injuring over 100 in Mumbai in 2003. On 6 August 2009, the special POTA court convicted the three accused and sentenced them to death.[1]

---

[1] Source- https://www.thehindu.com/news/national/Death-sentence-upheld-in-Mumbai-blasts-case/article13302108.ece.

FOUR

Prakash Chauhan and his wife Vidya's baby was stolen from Sir J.J. Hospital in 2003. When I met them seven years later, the couple had not given up hope. Every year on 12 January, they cut a cake at home to celebrate their son's birthday. They had lost their baby just two days after he was born. The child went missing from the maternity ward and though a police complaint was filed, nothing came of it. The couple, who lives in Dongri with their two children, is hopeful that one day they will find their child.

In 2010, six back-to-back cases of children being kidnapped were reported in Mumbai, raising serious concerns over the security of children. The city was reeling from the fear of kidnappers who walked away with children from railway stations, government hospitals and streets.

Some government hospitals banned burkhas in the maternity ward, when CCTV footage in one of the cases showed a woman wearing a burkha walking away with a baby that was not her own. The authorities were under tremendous pressure to solve the cases, because in 2010 apart from Delhi, Mumbai witnessed the highest number of crimes against children in the country.

According to the National Crime Records Bureau (NCRB), over 60,000 children go missing every year in India—that's one child every eight minutes. Of these, on an average, more than 22,000 are not found. Most of these children are abducted by gangs involved in trafficking. Over 2,00,000 children are listed as missing in India.

According to the NCRB, crimes against children showed a significant increase of 13.6 per cent (1,06,958) in 2016 over (94,172) 2015; kidnapping and abduction of children accounted for 52.3 per cent of the cases. Stories of kidnappings made headlines every alternate day in the newspapers. Though the cops made a few arrests, they had no clue about the kingpins.

I chased this story for almost four years, but due to lack of adequate information it remained untold for a very long time.

December 2014

The *Mid-Day* office

After an edit meeting, my boss and the then editor of *Mid-Day*, Sachin Kalbag, called me into his cabin and asked me to relook into the kidnapping story. He asked me to take my time but make sure it was a story that would be worth the effort.

Though the investigators had cracked a few cases of baby thefts, they had only ended up arresting the abductors. The motive remained unclear and no effort had been made to delve deeper into the recurrence of the crime with such frequency.

For starters, I tapped all the sources and informers in my phonebook. No one had any helpful inputs or tips for me. Even the cops couldn't give me a lead. Though they had rescued some children, they didn't know anything about the masterminds behind the racket. There was not a single person on my contact list whom I had not reached out to. The assignment had started making me anxious. I had become convinced that I wouldn't be able to find out more about the cases. After reaching out to almost every person who was directly or indirectly related to the story, I was finally put in touch with Prakash and Vidya.

Research

I had a hunch that the babies and children abducted were being used by crooks who employed children as beggars. Sadly, many end up begging on the streets and railway platforms with amputated limbs. A month earlier, I had worked on a tip-off about a similar mafia ring operating on the platforms of the Central Railway line near Ambarnath railway station.

One of the police *khabris* had tipped me off that the kingpin of this racket had accommodated dozens of children in one of the shanties close to the station. Every morning, kids were released on the platform. The boss kept an eye on them from a distance. They would assign a certain amount for the children to collect based on their age and experience. Once the amount was collected, the kids were asked to report to the kingpin who would then escort them back to their rooms. He ensured that the kids kept changing their locations every week. By the time I tracked down one of their accommodations, but they had left the place and were untraceable thereafter. I chased the story for almost a week but then the informer in the case vanished as well.

The other reason behind the kidnappings could possibly be related to illegal adoption. There were reports that the government had made the adoption process more rigorous. After making a few calls to shelter homes, I found out that legally adopting a child is a long-drawn process, where the potential parents' eligibility is tested at every step. It requires many documents, such as residence proof, bank account statements, photographs of the couple, medical certificates, tests, which include HIV tests, salary slips, three letters of guarantee from friends, two doctors' certificates, one letter from a guardian and a letter from a family member promising to take care of the child if the parents passed away before the child turned eighteen.

First, the couple is asked whether they would prefer to adopt a boy or a girl. Then, they are asked to submit the above documents. A social worker visits their house and interviews them to gauge the authenticity of their claims and to know if they would be good parents. After the social worker's approval, the couple is allowed to adopt a child.

The age of the child depends on the age of the parents. It was at the sole discretion of the charity organization. If the couple didn't want the child, they would have to provide ample reason why they were saying no. The organization ensures that the child has gone through all medical tests. The couple is asked to get the child tested by their own doctor for further assurance. Then the legal process begins and it takes at least three months for the couple to take their child home.

Groundwork

I began digging for information at government hospitals on the outskirts of Mumbai. At some hospitals I posed as a parent and at other places I pretended to be a social worker. After two days of visiting the maternity ward of a municipal hospital in Ulhasnagar, a town in Thane district, I stopped a ward boy to learn more.

I asked about a doctor and when he couldn't volunteer any information, I told him I was looking for a doctor who could help me with the surrogacy process. Eventually, as he began talking, I asked him what happened to unwanted babies in case parents refused to take them home and whether I could adopt one such baby. 'And what makes you think that I can help you?' he asked, scanning me from top to bottom.

'I am seeking help wherever possible,' I said. He shook his head and began to walk away. Before he left, he added, 'Why don't you check with the shelter homes around this area? Lots of stories keep floating around about their activities.'

I was not sure whether to take this man seriously. I inquired with the shopkeepers around the area about the orphanage and figured out that there was a shelter home close by, called Ulhasnagar Shelter Home.

This time I decided to prepare a bit before visiting. Going without a valid reason could jeopardize my investigations.

I told my editor Sachin about the development in the story and he gave me the go-ahead. It was decided that Shubha Shetty, the then editor of the Hitlist (Bollywood) section at *Mid-Day* would accompany me for the story, posing as my wife. We would visit the shelter home on the pretext of adopting a baby and record all the evidence on the hidden camera.

A Few Days Later

It had taken us almost half a day to reach the shelter home. After almost a week's research on the adoption process and orphanages in the city, we had chosen this one because it was in a more secluded area and thus, we thought, more likely to engage in illegal activities.

'Look at him. He is very obedient. You don't have to worry about his behaviour, he is very well mannered. In case you want to go for the shorter one (pointing to another boy), he is also very decent. He was brought to our home almost a year ago,' said a man sitting in a 200-square-foot government office, filled with old-fashioned wooden chairs and tables. The small office was adorned with portraits of several national heroes and a poster of a toddler that read, 'Bacche Bhagwan Ka Roop Hai' (Children are the image of God). But the way children were being paraded in front of us painted a different picture.

Rotating a marble paperweight on the table the manager continued, 'You are the fifth set of parents this week. Last week we gave away a child who had been staying here for the past seven years,' he said, with no sign of emotional attachment. It was hard for Shubha and me to believe the way the kids were being shopped around by the caretakers of this orphanage. It was heart-wrenching to see small children being paraded in front of us. Had there been no risk of jeopardizing our endeavour, we would have walked out immediately.

After showing us six boys, the man got up from his seat to walk towards a Godrej cupboard in one corner of the room. He removed a set of cardboard files and dropped them on the table with a loud thump. He asked his staff to produce another set of children. Boys in the age group of six to eight years stood in front of us. They were first asked to sit, stand and walk to prove to us that they were physically fit. Throughout our conversation, the kids stood stiffly in front of us. It broke our hearts to see them that way.

During this second parade, I told the man that we wanted infants or toddlers and not grown-up boys. He was clearly upset that we had not specified the age group earlier. Without wasting a minute, he yelled out to his staff to take the boys inside, trying hard to suppress his anger.

'It is not as easy as you think. There is a tedious government procedure involved. It will take you several years and you still won't find the child of your choice. Getting older boys would be much easier as would be looking after them. You don't have to do round-the-clock parenting,' he said. 'I am really sorry, you are at the wrong place,' he added, hinting for us to leave. Since it was getting dark, Shubha and I decided to call it a day and follow up the next morning.

However, a man who was watching us talking to his sahib quietly followed us as we made an exit. He was the same person who had escorted the kids in. Somehow, I sensed that he had something to share. Pretending to be unaware that he was following us, I asked Shubha to keep walking in the direction of an auto stand a few metres away from the shelter home's gate. The man started walking in a different direction, but the way he kept looking at us, I gauged that he wanted us to stop him.

'Bhau, konchya gavach tumhee?' (Where are you from?) I asked him in Marathi. He answered that he had been born and brought up in Mumbai. I thought I would try to strike up a conversation with a lie that I was also from somewhere close to his home town but his answer gave me no opening. I shot another query, 'Mumbai madhe kuthe?' asking where in the city he grew up. The man answered that he lived somewhere close to the orphanage. I tried to keep him talking and told him some false details about myself. But the man answered to the point. I was not sure whether it was the right choice but with nothing materializing at that point, I thought I should take a chance. So, I exchanged numbers with him and invited him for a drink.

For a few days, I kept in touch with this man over the phone on some pretext or the other. On the weekend, I finally invited him for a drink and he readily agreed. That was the first time he opened up and spoke about how corruption was rampant in not just his but all the other orphanages in and around Thane. Foodgrains and pulses donated to the ashram would find their way to the kitchens of staffers. As the booze went down, the man went on about orphanages and malpractices. But unfortunately, he had no information about what I was looking for. My second lead had also fallen through. Before leaving, he assured me that he would look for someone who would help us with an alternative route to adoption.

First Breakthrough

For almost a week I did not hear from the man. I could see that the story was falling apart. I avoided making eye contact with my editor out of embarrassment and eventually decided I would end my search. But a few days later, the man from the orphanage called on my cell phone.

'Sahib, it's me. I want to tell you something important, it is better if you call me from the landline,' he said.

He had taken a lot of precautions during our earlier interactions. When we started talking to each other, he said he would not give me his name and made me promise that I would make no attempt to find out more about him. Since it was not important to the story, I agreed. He wanted to ensure that our conversation was secure and the phone was not being tapped, which is why he insisted I call him from the office landline on a random number.

He told me that when he was having a drink with a couple of friends from the nearby ashram, one of them had talked about a woman from the another ashram who was involved in finding babies for those who were willing to pay money. He told me this woman lived at an ashram for handicapped kids very close to the shelter we had already visited. Then he hurriedly cut the phone, saying he had to go. His call had me energized. After a short meeting with the editor and Shubha, we decided to make a second attempt and visit the ashram.

As we entered the gate of the ashram, a short woman wearing a cotton sari approached us. 'What do you want? Have you come for a donation?' she asked. 'No, tai, we want to adopt a child. Someone told us that you will be able to help us,' I replied. The woman did not like our upfront approach. 'Who told you so? You have the wrong information. I have no clue what you are talking about,' she said agitatedly.

'Let's go. Somebody has played a prank on us,' I told Shubha. Looking downcast, we both began to walk out of the gate. 'Wait,' she said. 'At least tell me who sent you to me?'

Instead of answering her question, I said, 'We don't know the man who sent us to you very well. Maybe he was playing a prank. Maybe he was not aware of what this means to us. This was the last hope. Sorry to bother you.' We then began walking towards the gate again.

'You have called me tai, I will surely want to help you out,' she said, following us eagerly. 'Your information was not wrong. I can help you but I need to have some reference. It is a matter of trust after all. Anyway, since you look genuine to me, I will help you. There is one child that was born a few weeks ago. The family is poor and they cannot take care of the baby,' she said.

I was surprised that the woman who had been reluctant to talk just a few moments ago was now readily agreeing to share so many details. Trying to control my excitement, I asked her how we would go about it.

Shubha pitched in, saying, 'We are so grateful to you. You are no less than god for us.'

'Don't get excited so soon. There is one condition,' said the woman. 'You will have to pay a good amount of money to the mother as compensation for keeping the child with you.' When she told us the amount, I paused, realizing it was too much for our office to spend that kind of money for the story. We negotiated with her, but she refused to bring down the amount.

To gain our confidence and divert the conversation from the price, the woman began to tell us about herself.

Her name was Vijaya Sonawane. She repeatedly said that she was not a fraud and could take us to see the child the next day. All we had to do was meet her near the municipal hospital in Ulhasnagar in the afternoon.

After reaching our office we discussed the story with our editor. In those days Rs 2.5 lakh, which is what she had asked for, was too much for a sting operation. I was sure that the story would get stuck again. But within a week, Sachin called me to his cabin and said, 'There is good news for you.'

Meanwhile, to convince Sonawane that we were genuinely interested, we met her the next day outside Central Hospital in Ulhasnagar, despite not knowing at the time if we would get approval for the amount that she had asked us for. She told us that another woman (probably an agent) who worked in a surrogacy clinic in Mulund would take us to the baby, who was in a slum in Ulhasnagar with his family. On our way there, Sonawane cautioned us not to speak to anyone about the money except her. She said she knew the 'right people' in court and could get the paperwork done in just a day. She even volunteered to be the guarantor.

She also claimed to be in touch with the doctors and ward officers at the municipal hospital. We were stunned that this woman who could barely read or write was managing such a huge network, including doctors and municipal staff. Sonawane kept boasting that this was not the first time she had facilitated something like this, saying, 'I have sold many babies to childless couples across Maharashtra and other states in the past.'

We waited together for her associate Ratna Ubale for almost three hours before Sonawane finally spoke about Ratna. Till then we had thought that Sonawane was the kingpin of the racket, but the way she was speaking about Ratna, it was clear that Ratna was heading the network.

We found out that Ubale was the conduit between the couples who wanted to give away their children and agents like Sonawane who helped find them homes. She kept an eye on government and private hospitals looking for unwed or poor mothers who would want to give away their babies. Ubale lured such mothers with the promise of paying them a couple of lakhs. She would keep a chunk of the money while the rest of the cash was shared by the agents. Sonawane was one of her favourite agents because she gave her the most business through childless couples who would visit the orphanage inquiring about the adoption procedure.

But as we spoke to Sonawane, we started to worry because Ubale refused to pick up her calls. I felt that something was amiss. Either the woman had become suspicious or she might have promised the baby to someone else. But Sonawane was confident that her friend would surely make it to the meeting. It was almost evening by now. But our wait confirmed that we were genuinely interested in the baby. However, the problem that I kept dwelling on was that the camera we were using could not capture images in the dark.

'I think we should plan for another day,' I finally said.

Not wanting to lose out on sealing the deal, Sonawane said, 'I will make one last call to her.' She had tried her best to keep us waiting by narrating stories of her village, husband and her association with Bollywood actor Nana Patekar, for whom she used to cook many years ago.

Finally, Ubale called. 'Chalo, didi,' Sonawane said looking at Shubha. She had called us near the Ulhasnagar railway station. As we reached near the station, we saw a tall woman waiting for us, accompanied by a short lady, who she claimed was her colleague.

'Didi, she is Ratna,' Sonawane said pointing towards the taller of the two. She had curly hair and a heavy Marathi accent. She greeted both of us with a smile, saying, 'Sorry, didi, aane mein thoda late hogaya' (I'm sorry, I got a little delayed). Ratna said that since it was already late, we should rush to the baby's house. On our way, she began introducing herself and told us about her work at the clinic in Mulund and how she had helped several couples to get a baby.

'Aap aao kabhi clinic mein mere' (Come to my clinic some day), she told us. On our way to the baby's home, Ratna dropped a hint that we could also go for a surrogate child and went on to elaborate the procedure followed by her clinic. She explained that if we opted for it, we would have to pay the mother Rs 2.45 lakh and bear her medical expenses. The total expenditure would be up to Rs 10 lakh. In less than ten minutes, Ratna had already made Sonawane uncomfortable. Fearing that she might try to poach her client, Sonawane interrupted. 'Let us have a look at the child first. The rest can keep happening. I think we should hurry up instead of wasting our time talking,' she said.

Ratna took us to a slum where the mother of the child was introduced to us. She lived with a big family—her husband, two children, sister, brother and others. She was apparently selling the child because she did not want it. Ratna boasted how she had dissuaded the mother from aborting the child so that she could make some money after the birth.

Here are some of the conversations recorded during our visit to the baby's home:

Shubha (after looking at the child): So cute!

Sonawane (comments on the baby's nose): Yacha naak bagitla ka, majya poori sarkha hai (Have you seen her nose, it is just like my daughter . . . referring to her granddaughter).

Bhupen: Iska wazan kitna hai (How much does the baby weigh)?

Sonawane: Dhai kilo (2.5 kg).

Ratna: Ata sukla tari nahi tar janamla tevha mast hota (The baby has become thin now but he was healthier at the time of his birth).

Sonawane: Mast zoplay na (He is sleeping so peacefully).

Shubha: Haan.

Sonawane: Baal bill mast hai na (Isn't his hair lovely).

Shubha: Haan.

We then proceeded to pose for pictures with the baby.

Ratna (explaining why the woman didn't want to keep the child): Ek ladka aur ek ladki hai usko (She has a son and a daughter).

Bhupen: Bahut achha, pyara bachcha hai (The child is very sweet).

We handed over Rs 101 as 'shagun' to the child's mother before leaving the house. We waited outside the door to listen to their conversation. Ratna and the baby's aunt were trying to persuade the mother to give it away. They were telling her that since she had planned to abort the child anyway, she should give it away and earn some money. Once outside, Sonawane warned us again not to discuss the deal in front of Ratna. To show herself to be one step ahead of Ratna, Sonawane told us we could also try an alternative of surrogacy through intercourse in case the deal did not come through.

Sonawane was still clearly irritated by Ratna as she continued to complain about her. She told us how Ratna had taken away a major portion of the fee meant for them by getting couples surrogate mothers. Sonawane revealed that she had housed one such surrogate mother whom Ratna had brought to her.

Sonawane added that Ratna received a commission of Rs 20,000 for every surrogate she brought. Apart from that, she would take Rs 2000 from the Rs 8000 paid to surrogate mothers every month by the couple. After the child was delivered, Ratna took Rs 50,000 from the total of Rs 2.5 lakh paid to the mother.

Surrogacy through Intercourse

Sonawane told us about a sordid case involving a woman who had conceived for a rich businessman. According to Sonawane, a builder from Alibaug had desperately wanted a son and had approached her because his wife had given birth to two sets of twin girls. Since she had to undergo C-sections both the times, he didn't want to risk her health again. The builder was reluctant to adopt or opt for in vitro fertilization. So Sonawane suggested that she could get a woman to stay with him and bear a child through natural intercourse. She claimed she had arranged for a woman from Nashik. The woman conceived with the wife's knowledge and consent. The builder bought the woman a flat to stay in for a while. At a sonography centre near Shirdi, where Sonawane claimed she had contacts, they discovered that the sex of the unborn baby was male. According to Sonawane, the woman was now six months pregnant and being looked after by the builder's wife.

Yeh Haath Mein Paisa, Yeh Haath Mein Bachcha

A day later, we visited Sonawane to hand over the first instalment of Rs 60,000. She asked us not to come the next day for the remaining amount. 'It's a Saturday, not an auspicious day to take the child home,' she explained. She asked us to give the amount at the earliest though and take the baby and the documents. I tried to negotiate with her once again.

Bhupen: Mausi, do me bitha do na (Please try settling it in Rs 2 lakh).

Sonawane: Nahi, do mein nahi, woh log bolte hai un logo ke paas doosri party hai (No, I can't do it for Rs 2 lakh. They are saying they have another interested party).

Bhupen: Baki ka paisa de diya to turant bachcha de denge (Will we get the child as soon as we hand over the balance money)?

Sonawane: Yeh haath mein paisa, yeh haath mein bachcha. (You can give the money with one hand and take the child with the other).

Sonawane (talking about Ratna): Uss din phone pe didi (Shubha) ne sab suna. Usko boli medical report sab poora kaam karke deneka. Mummy ka bhi report aur uska bhi report. Woh bol rahi thi kal hi paper banao. Maine to kal hi stamp paper lekar rakh liya tha. Vakil bola mein notary karke de deta hu. Vakil to apna aadmi hai. Usko main fees ek mahine baad degi. Itna to vishwas hain na vakil ka (That day Didi heard everything she (Ratna) said. I have told her to give all the medical papers, including the reports of the baby and her mother. I have already bought the stamp paper and the advocate has agreed to do the notary. The advocate knows me well. Even if I pay him next month, he will be fine with it).

Bhupen: Aur kuch thoda bahut kum to karega na (He will reduce the money a little, I hope).

Sonawane: Main tumko kya bola, 30,000 mein khud dungi tumko apne taraf se. Mereko tum che mahine mein do, itna vishwas hai mereko. Main government servant hoon, aisi vaisi raste wali aurat thodi hi hoon. Nashik mein tum mera flat dekho, ghar dekho. Tumko yakin nahi aayega. Tumko do bees (Rs 2,20,000) lana hoga poora (What did I tell you? I will give Rs 30,000 from my side and you can pay me back in six months. I trust you. I am a government servant. You should see my house in Nashik, you won't believe it. You will have to bring Rs 2,20,000).

Bhupen: 60,000 diya na . . . toh aur mereko aapko dena hai 1,60,000 (I have given you Rs 60,000 . . . so now I have to give you Rs 1,60,000).

Sonawane: Haan.

Bhupen: Matlab abhi maine aapko yeh paisa diya, aap kisi aur ko bachcha nahi dikhaogi (This means after I give you this money, you won't show the child to anyone else).

As per Sonawane's instructions, we went to Ulhasnagar to hand over the remaining amount of Rs 1.6 lakh. There, she took the money and said, 'Get your identity proofs on Tuesday and I will see to it that your paperwork is done.' After about four hours, the child was handed over to us with his medical reports, along with a casual remark that we should take care of it. Sonawane asked for another Rs 10,000 which we paid her, bringing the total to Rs 2.3 lakh.

After that, we approached a government-run organization, Childline, whose officials approached the

Child Welfare Committee (CWC), which then helped us admit the baby to the Vishwa Balak Kendra orphanage in Nerul. This was accomplished with the help of social worker Sharad Barse, who works with Aasra Childline in Kalyan. We gave a copy of the videos recorded during the sting to Barse. The evidence was to be submitted to the CWC.

Racket Unearthed

The article was read widely. Soon after the story got published in *Mid-Day*, the authorities came under pressure. The CWC took serious cognizance of the article and requested me to produce evidence before it. Once the evidence was submitted, the cops were involved and they were forced to register an offence of child trafficking against the accused. In less than a week, the cops arrested four people in the case, including the parents of the baby. Several news channels and online news portals ran stories of the operation, and congratulated the newspaper for the exposé. The state minister for women and child development not only assured that the strictest action would be taken but also promised to make the adoption process simpler and more transparent for couples to prevent such cases in the future. All the accused have been chargesheeted in the court and the case is still on trial.

FIVE

Over the course of my career, I've realized that most things in this world can have a rip-off. Even dons. But fake dons can be scary too. This sting began when I was introduced to Khota Shakeel. Not Chhota, but Khota. The moment I heard his name, I remember feeling cornered and scared, fully aware of the danger that my job entailed. In the beginning of December 2012, I experienced a rare phase when I did not have a big crime story to cover. During such phases, reporters utilize their time to keep in touch with their sources.

One such afternoon, I went to meet one of the most resourceful people I knew, Ashraf Khan, who had become a dear friend. Ashraf, a man of his word, had always been lucky for me. His network in the pockets of south

Mumbai was all because of his goodwill. There wasn't a single lane or apartment in the Muslim-dominated pockets of south Mumbai where people didn't know him or look up to him. Like the city, he too never slept at night. According to Ashraf, that was the best time to connect with people. He would say, 'I haven't slept at night for the last twenty years.' Growing up hearing about how dons and gangsters conducted business at night, he had mastered the art of being out and about at that time, too. All this had gained him some fans.

It had been a very long time since I had met Ashraf. He asked me to come to a travel agency that helped people procure visas to go on hajj or other work in the Middle East. I reached the office on time, where a man greeted me and asked me to take a seat till Ashraf arrived. He offered me water and ensured that I was not left unattended.

Ashraf soon entered the room and welcomed me with his regular salutation, 'Bhai, tum ho kidhar' (Where have you been)? Ashraf gestured to the man who had kindly offered me water and introduced him saying, 'Inse milo, yeh hai [This is] Shakeel Ahmed Shaikh.' I got up from my seat and shook hands with him. After a long pause, Ashraf looked at me and said, 'Alias Khota Shakeel.'

I was confused, so I asked, 'Kya?' The name Khota Shakeel had sent shivers down my spine. Why was Ashraf introducing me to him? Had I trusted the wrong guy? Why would he make me meet someone dangerous? I started looking for a way to escape that small office but the door was too far and the other two were sitting close to me.

Two months ago, I had boasted to Ashraf about my article on Ahmed, written from information by martyr and encounter specialist Vijay Salaskar, who was killed in the 26 November 2008 terror attack. Salaskar had told me how Ahmed, who was good at mimicking underworld don Chhota Shakeel, would call people for extortion while sharing the same roof with Shakeel.

A high-profile builder in Mumbai had even paid him a hefty sum, fooled by his mimicry. A few days later, when Chhota Shakeel himself called up, the bewildered builder said that he had already paid the money. That is how Shakeel Ahmed got the name 'Khota'. His father was employed at Chhota Shakeel's office at Temkar Street in Bhendi Bazaar. He fled from India, along with Shakeel's most trusted aide, Fahim Machmach. I had been the first one to report on Khota and his activities in *Mid-Day*, and the smirk on his face showed that he was well aware of it.

Seeing how nervous I was, Ahmed and Ashraf started laughing. 'Bhai, he is my friend just like you. You don't have to worry about anything. Calm down,' Ashraf said. I shook hands with Ahmed again, who offered me another glass of water and gave me some time to settle down. In just a few minutes, Ahmed turned out to be very different from what I had heard about him. He cracked jokes and shared interesting details of the time he had spent with Shakeel.

While we were chatting, there was a knock on the door. Two burkha-clad women entered, asking whether marriages were conducted at the office. It was very weird for someone to barge into a travel office with such an unusual query. Ashraf asked the two women to come inside and take a seat. After offering them water, he asked them what exactly they were looking for.

One of them said, 'We have come from Hyderabad. For almost a week, we have been searching for someone who can help us marry Arabs.'

'And who told you that this travel agency will be able to help you?' Ashraf asked the woman.

'Some agent with whom we were in touch till two days ago said that a travel agency in Dongri is helping girls find Arab grooms,' she said. Ashraf looked at me, mirroring what I had already been thinking—this could be a good story for my newspaper. Ashraf ordered tea for the women and they told us more about the network.

Some people in the city, acting as agents, co-ordinated with Muslim women across the country who were looking to make money. The agents were in touch with maulvis in Mumbai who were approached by Arab men for temporary marriages. Because these Arab men believed that prostitution was against Islam, they would marry a woman during their stay in India and pay them a hefty amount. The woman was expected to take care of all their household chores and maintain a sexual relationship with the man. Before leaving the country, the man would separate from the woman by verbally giving triple talaq and make the balance payment. The opportunity of quick money had been luring several young girls to Mumbai.

The price usually varied from Rs 15,000 to nearly Rs 1 lakh for a ten-day marriage. Girls from poor families were forced into marriage with the Arabs, many of whom arrived on tourist visas from Saudi Arabia, UAE, Iran, Oman, Kuwait and Qatar. This form of flesh trade carried on under the veneer of nikah. Abusing the sanctioned provision which allows a Muslim man to have four wives at a time, many old Arabs not only married minors in Mumbai and Hyderabad, but also more than one minor in a single trip to the country.

For as little as Rs 2000 per job, scores of women would come to Mumbai every day, hoping to catch the eye of an adulterous tourist. The qazi who officiated the wedding and facilitated the divorce proceedings would take 50 per cent of the negotiated price as his cut. The agent who sourced the girls would take 25 per cent of the balance amount. The pimps, cab drivers and sub-agents would charge Rs 500–1000 per deal. How much did the girls get?

The women who had landed up at the travel office did not know who to contact. Some people claiming to be agents had cheated them on the pretext of arranging meetings with maulvis. We assured the women that we were in no way linked to the racket. Once they had finished their tea, they left.

The Victims

I began with some basic research on Arab nationals visiting Mumbai and I noticed that there were specific hotels that they seemed to frequent. I met some of waiters and staff in these hotels to get information about their activities. After meeting a series of informers and residents, I got my first lead outside two hotels in south Mumbai—Hotel Rajdoot and Pals Hotel.

Ashraf and I approached two burkha-clad women who were emerging from Hotel Rajdoot, which was a popular destination for Arabs. 'As-salam alaykum,' Ashraf greeted one of them. The woman smiled and replied, 'Alaykum salaam.' She looked at Ashraf with amusement and asked, 'Have we met earlier?' To keep the woman distracted with the conversation, Ashraf said, 'Mujhe bhi aisa laga' (Even I think so). He managed to charm the women, who said they were Razia and Shazia, and continued to chat with us for a couple of hours. We even exchanged numbers before leaving. Ashraf told me it was not advisable to ask for details on the first meeting, so he was working to gain their confidence. After a few days of talking over the phone, the women decided to meet Ashraf because they thought that he was an agent who would help them find Arab grooms. I'm glad Ashraf was helping me out even though there was no immediate tangible benefit in it for him. He probably did it because he wanted to keep up a rapport with me, but I was grateful for the help in any case.

At the second meeting, Razia told us that they were residents of Hyderabad and had come to Mumbai in search of agents. After hunting for agents for nearly a week, they had run out of cash and made up their minds to return home. Throughout our conversation with Razia, her friend Shazia waited outside the tea stall we had met at, talking to her family members. After Razia escorted her inside, she sobbed constantly. As we tried to console her, Shazia revealed that she wanted to go back home.

Ashraf and I were moved. He took some money from his pocket and handed it over to one of them, saying, 'I hope this will be of some help to you. Take care of your family. Allah takes care of everyone. Dua mein yaad rakhna' (Remember me in prayers).

Through the two girls we met another girl, Mumtaz, in a hotel in Dongri in south Mumbai posing as an agent, who had more details of how the network functioned. Mumtaz had met an Arab man just a few days ago who wanted to take her to Saudi Arabia by performing nikah, but she had refused as she did not trust him. She had heard many stories of Indian women being taken to Arab countries and made sex slaves. They were made to do all the household chores and satisfy the men in bed. Mumtaz had been in the city for a long time and had met a series of agents and Arabs. She was looking for an Arab groom since she had run out of cash and had been asked to leave her temporary accommodation.

According to Mumtaz, a week before she met us, she had personally witnessed three nikahs. The first was done for Rs 35,000 for fifteen days and the second for Rs 14,000 for ten days. But the real shock was the third one where a fifteen-year-old girl from Hyderabad had been married to a senior Arab national for Rs 1 lakh. However, Mumtaz refused to share the details of agents.

The Maulvis

After having toiled for nearly twenty days, I had a breakthrough in the case. This time, one of my informers took me to the address of a qazi at Do Tanki, near Nagpada, who performed nikahs of girls with Arabs.

At the entrance of the dingy lane, we saw a board for Qazi Mohammad Zakaria Oamar, known as Chief Qazi of Mumbai. He was a grey-haired man, whom all the visitors called 'Qazi Sahib'. There was a line of burkha-clad women outside his office, most of whom were looking for Arab grooms.

It was almost like a darbar. He was busy conversing with one of the girls when we entered. Upon seeing us, Zakaria pulled down his specs to the edge of his nose and asked 'Boliye, janab?' Before we could reply, he picked up a metal box from the wooden table on his side, removed a paan from it and put it in his mouth. We told him that one of our female friends wanted to marry an Arab and asked if he would help her find a groom.

Ashraf: Unko (female friend) bula loon kal (Should I call her tomorrow)?

Zakaria: Jumma baad mein (After Friday prayers).

Ashraf: Masla aisa hai ki unko yaha ka koi nahi chahiye (The issue is that she doesn't want an Indian).

Zakaria: Theek hai, kal jumma baad aao (Okay, come after prayers tomorrow).

Ashraf: Aapka naam (Your name)?

Zakaria: Mohammad Zakaria Oamar. Passport hai? Passport to nahi hoga (Does she have a passport)?

Bhupen: Passport hai na (Yes, she has a passport).

Zakaria: Jayegi bahar shaadi karke (Will she go abroad after marriage)?

Bhupen: Nahi, woh char din ka mamla hota hai na (No, but what about the short-term marriages?) Hai kya aisa koi zehen mein (Is there any such matter in mind)?

Zakaria: Haan, hai to (Yes, there is).

Ashraf: Theek hai, teen baje aate hai kal (Okay, we will come at 3 p.m. tomorrow).

I then involved the paper and told the people concerned at work of the lead I had been following. A female reporter would have to pose as the bride looking for Arab grooms. The assignment was risky and some of my colleagues flatly refused, considering the threat involved. But one person was ready to take on the challenge. It was our education correspondent, Kranti Vibhute. Without giving it a second thought, Kranti agreed to do the assignment. After a brief chat, we decided that she would pretend to be Shabnam, a poor girl from a Hyderabad-based Muslim family. We chose Hyderabad as most girls involved in this racket seemed to be from that city. We asked Kranti to wear a burkha and took her to meet the qazi. By that time, in 2012, there was an ample variety of spy cameras, available in all forms of daily wear, such as tie pins, spectacles, umbrellas and caps. We chose one which was hidden in a watch.

Zakaria opened up at our meeting, giving us more inside details of the trade. He said that the easy availability of women for Arabs had spoilt them. Hotel Rajdoot and Pals Hotel at Cotton Green had turned into dens for such activities, where women queued up every evening, hoping to be picked by Arabs.

He said that it was due to this abundance in choice that the rates the men paid had fallen drastically. The women who went on a khadama visa, which is for domestic help, were increasingly being exploited by Arabs. The women would be hired as contract labour and the Arabs would sexually exploit them.

The following is part of the conversation that took place:

Zakaria: Bambai ki hai (referring to Shabnam) (Is she from Mumbai)?

Bhupen: Mumbra ki.

Zakaria: Bahar nahi jayegi? (Won't you go abroad)?

Shabnam shook her head.

Ashraf: Kuwari hai (She's a virgin).

Zakaria: Kunwari ke liye jab koi shaadi wala aayega tab hoga (Marriages for virgins only take place when someone who wants a virgin shows up).

On realizing that he might have misunderstood us, we changed our statement and claimed that we wanted to find an Arab groom for her.

Zakaria: Party aati hai tab baat hoti hai. Saamne saamne. Do din mein aa jayenge. Hum logo ne Arbon ko bigaad ke rakha hua hai. Rajdoot aur Pals hotel mein shaam ke waqt aise hi ladkiyan bhari padi hoti hai. Woh dedh hazaar, do hazaar mein rehne ke liye tayyar hai. Unka mijaz bigad diya hai. Jab unko dedh hazaar mein milega to mere paas kyu ayenge? Ab woh pehle waali baat nahi rahi. Zyada karke sab cheez apna bhaav gira diye (Discussions take place face-to-face when parties arrive. We have spoiled the Arabs. Every evening women like this can be found at Rajdoot and Pals hotels. They are ready to stay for Rs 1500-2000. Their nature has been ruined. When they can get someone for Rs 1500 then why will they come to me? It isn't like it was before.)

Bhupen (referring to Arabs): Lekin kitna waqt lagega? Aate rehte hai aapke paas (How long will it take? Do they keep coming to you)?

Zakaria: Aate hi rehte hai. Aa gaye to line se aagaye, kabhi kabhi do-do din nahi aate (They keep coming. Sometimes there's a line, sometimes there's no one for a few days).

Bhupen: Lekin mahine bhar se pehle hoga (Will it be done in a month)?

Zakaria: Mahine bhar se pehle hi ho jayega. Jaise ayenge phone karunga, ghanta do ghanta pehle (Yes. I will call a few hours before they come).

Shabnam: Lekin khula ho jayega na?

Bhupen: Woh pooch rahi hai talaq ho jayega na (She's asking whether the divorce will happen or not)?

Zakaria: Arey woh salaam de ke chale jaate hai (They just say goodbye and leave).

Bhupen: Talaq ke liye idhar hi aate hai (Do they come here for the divorce)?

Zakaria: Zaban se bol diya, ho gaya (They just say the words and it is done).

Zakaria's phone rang and he spoke with someone in Arabic. From his conversation, it was evident that he had struck a deal with an Arab. It was probably to facilitate a meeting between the man on the phone and the women who had met Zakaria before us. When the call ended, he took his leave. From his behaviour it was clear that he was expecting someone important. As we left, we saw a tall Arab man entering the lane. A couple of women followed him, and they entered the office.

This meeting could be crucial evidence for the story. We could not pass up this chance. I turned towards Zakaria's office, trying hard to think of an excuse for going back. I reached his doorstep and drew back the curtain. They paused when they saw me and Zakaria asked 'Ji, janab?' I told him that I had left cell phone behind and began looking for it. As I searched the room, I discreetly took a few photos and videos of the room with my hidden camera and walked out without raising any suspicion. Once I had exited, Ashraf and I decided to hang around in the area, thinking we might find more clues.

After almost half an hour, the Arab man emerged from the lane and began walking away. Only one of the two women who had gone in emerged from the room and followed about ten to fifteen feet behind. We tailed them, keeping enough distance not to be seen. After walking for about half a kilometre, the Arab and the woman looked around the street and then began walking hand in hand. It looked like the marriage had been fixed. We saw them entering a restaurant in each other's arms. Ashraf and I waited on the opposite side for a while, discussing our next step. Suddenly, I saw the same man emerging from the building.

We were hardly twelve feet away. The man looked at me and stopped. He stared for a few moments with eyes wide open and then charged towards me. I began talking to Ashraf, pretending that everything was normal. Ashraf was unaware of the man's presence as he was facing me. 'Niklo' (Leave), I mouthed to Ashraf, and we began walking in the opposite direction. For a second, our pursuer got confused, but then continued chasing me. As I increased my speed and started turning into tiny lanes, the Arab followed me. Once again, I pretended to be calm and stopped at a paan shop. I was scared that the man would attack me at any moment. I was sure I wouldn't be able to put up a fight and tried hard to control my fear.

But suddenly, the Arab changed his mind and began walking in the opposite direction, leaving me bewildered. While I was trying to gauge the reason for his reaction, I saw a police van waiting at a distance. Thankfully, their presence had helped me. Without wasting a minute, I took a cab straight to my office.

The Final Take

We called up Qazi Zakaria the next day to find out if he had received any suitable proposals for Shabnam. Zakaria called us to his office, informing us that some Arabs were about to visit him in a while and that we should bring Shabnam with us, so that the bride and groom could see each other. We could not afford to go wrong here. This would give us the evidence needed to print this story. Before leaving our office, Kranti and I rehearsed to make sure we were on the same page. I had asked Kranti to give me a puzzled look whenever she had no answers for whatever the Arabs or Zakaria asked. This was also going to be one of the riskiest moments of the operation. There were lots of ifs and buts for which we had no answers. We had no idea of the number of people that were going to be present and we were not prepared in case any of the men chose Kranti. I called Ashraf and informed him about Zakaria's call to reach his office on short notice. 'Dost ko lekar aana' (Bring your friend), I told him over the phone. 'Who is this friend?' Kranti asked me. To avoid the question, I pretended to receive a call.

Earlier, Ashraf and I had decided on some secret code words. 'Dost' was the code word for his licensed revolver, which he almost always carried on him. I did not want to tell Kranti this since it would lead to unnecessary panic. We picked up Ashraf and reached Zakaria's office. When we entered the room, we saw three Arab men sitting along with three girls, the qazi and an assistant. After Kranti took a seat, she was asked to remove her niqab for the Arabs to have a look at her. I had told Ashraf that in case any Arab chose Kranti, we would take her out on the pretext of buying her something and escape. Also, if anything went wrong, he would use his 'dost' to scare off people.

The Arabs looked at the girls and asked us questions in Arabic, which were translated for us by Zakaria.

Arab 1: First, tell me your relationship with this girl?

Arab 2: Are you married to her? Is she married?

Bhupen: She is a friend.

Kranti was a bit taken aback at the line of questioning. I was scared that they would actually choose her. But we chose to stay calm and wait till they said anything. The men continued asking more questions. After the sixth one, one of the Arab men shifted his focus to another girl.

Arab 3: What is her name? How old is she?

Zakaria interrupted the Arab and whispered something in his ear, then added: There are the three girls. There are five girls in all. But you see these now. One girl is from Grant Road, one from Bombay Central.

After a discussion with the Arabs, Zakaria informed one of the girls in her mid-twenties that the man had chosen her. This is what he said:

Zakaria: Udhar mat dekh, idhar dekh (Don't look there, look here).

Woman: Kitna (How much)?

Zakaria: Rs 14,000. Itni der se baitha hai bechara, karle shaadi (The poor guy has been sitting for so long, just marry him).

One of the three Arabs got agitated and asked the three girls to leave.

Zakaria (to the Arabs): Give the girls Rs 500 for their troubles.

Woman: Kitne din ke liye (For how many days)?

Zakaria (shouts at the girl): Bol diya. Samajhti nahi tu. Jab bolu to samajh jaya kar. Ho gaya (I've already said it. You should understand when I talk. It is done).

The Arab then pulled out two notes of Rs 500 and handed one to Shabnam and one to the other girl who had been rejected.

We found out that a taxi driver had been involved in the deal too. As we waited outside the qazi's office we saw a driver accompany the girl chosen to be married. He took her to a cab parked close to Zakaria's office and was soon followed by the Arab who had chosen her.

We were relieved he had chosen another girl over Kranti and the story ended without any more adventure. We took Zakaria's leave and asked him to get back to us in case he came across new grooms, though we had no plan to chase the story further, as we had collected enough evidence on our camera.

The next day, the article covered almost the entire edition of the paper. People called to congratulate me, and the online article had a record number of readers that day. The police swung into action and rushed a team to Zakaria's office. All the agents and other maulvis in the area went underground, and there was no sign of related activity in the city. The Crime Branch officials set up a team to chase Zakaria, but he disappeared from the city and never returned. The then (late) joint commissioner of police Himanshu Roy went on record to congratulate *Mid-Day* for its outstanding work.

Meanwhile, the articles had also added a feather to Ashraf's cap. People recognized him for his work. Some called to say that he was working against the community, but many congratulated him for helping us expose the network. In the end, through his network, Ashraf found out that girls who came to the city to find Arab grooms had gone back to their home towns.

SIX

I was on one of my visits to D.B. Marg police station in south Mumbai, sharing a cup of tea with a police officer at a roadside chai stall. I was on Lamington Road, which is known as a hub of computer hardware in the city, and noticed a huge crowd outside Dream Land and Imperial theatres. In 2008, when Internet on mobile phones was not as prevalent or affordable, access to online porn was limited. As a result, most people thronged theatres on Lamington Road for every new C-grade film, which often had soft porn scenes. This sort of cinema, which operates parallel to Bollywood, is supposed to be worth at least one-fourth of the net worth of India's mainstream film industry, which was estimated at 50 billion in 2018.

Pointing to a poster, the officer told me, 'The crowd at this theatre has become a headache for the duty officers as the craze for these movies is insane. Whether it's a weekday or a weekend, the numbers are constant.'

The officer, who had served a couple of months at DB Marg, told me that these movies were a big boost for the business in the Congress House and Kamathipura red light areas. Many among the audience would head straight to the sex workers afterwards to satisfy their urges.

Sensing the possibility of a story, I hurried to Imperial Cinema after my meeting to find out why these films were generating such interest. But as I walked towards the ticket counter, many people told me the morning show had sold out, in just a few hours.

As I reached the gate, I saw a huge crowd gathered to watch the show. Most of them were hamals (cart pullers or labourers doing odd jobs in the city) and people who had emigrated from other towns to Mumbai in search of work. Surprisingly, I also spotted many senior citizens, some of whom were carrying bags of groceries.

The front of the theatre had a huge poster of a movie called *Be Parda*. It had a woman wearing a red gown that prominently displayed her cleavage. Positioned around her were photographs of other lovemaking scenes with different co-stars in seductive poses. To attract customers, the theatre staff had put up posters of the same artist in two different coloured bikinis at the entrance of the theatre. I decided to try for a ticket for the afternoon show, which would be two hours later. Despite it being just ten in the morning, there was a large crowd at the counter. The way men were rushing to buy tickets, I doubted I would get a chance to see the show.

As the ticket counter opened for the later show, the queue went berserk. People piled on to each other, hoping to get to the front, only to realize that the show was full. Seeing the rush, I decided to give up and started walking away. As I was leaving the theatre, I saw a distant relative waiting on the other side of the road. He was at the bus stop a few metres away from the theatre. As our eyes met, I hurried away, hoping he had not recognized me. I belonged to a community in which boys are married by the age of twenty-three, but I had managed to avoid it till my late twenties. I didn't want my parents to think I was one of the people who was desperate to watch one of these movies at 10 a.m. on a weekday. It would only start off the discussion about finding me a wife all over again.

Almost a week later, I noticed an unusual change in my family's behaviour. My mother usually brings me tea in bed every morning but now even after twenty minutes of waking up, she hadn't done so. Despite asking her the reason many times, she refused to respond. I was bewildered.

I got dressed and went to the living room, but before I could take a seat in front of my father, my mother put down a cup of tea on the table. She cleared her throat while leaving the room, hinting to my father that he should talk to me about something. I thought it was one of the regular discussions about getting married but from my father's body language I gauged that it was something else.

'Beta, I know that you are in no hurry to get married,' he said. 'But what is driving you to see those dirty movies in such cheap theatres? What will people think about you and us?' he said.

On the pretext of picking up the cup, my mother came back into the living room. 'Ganda, ganda picture joi che' (You watch bad films), she said before going back to the kitchen.

A few days later, I made another attempt to watch a movie. This time I decided to go to another theatre, called New Shirin on Saat Rasta in Nagpada. I covered my face with a muffler and cap before standing in the queue to buy a ticket.

The theatre was running a movie called *Main Cabrewali*, starring lookalikes of Shatrughan Sinha and Prem Chopra. I chatted with some of the people milling around who seemed to be regulars and learnt that it was an old movie and thus unable to draw large crowds. Only a few people had come to watch it.

I chose a seat in one of the last rows. There were hardly thirty people in the cinema hall. Half an hour into the movie, I was stunned to see a woman enter the theatre. At first I thought a family had entered the hall accidentally. Fifteen minutes later, when a lovemaking scene between the lookalike Shatrughan Sinha and his co-star began, the woman got up from her seat and began moving around the theatre. She would stop and stand beside certain seats. I asked a man sitting beside me who she was and he told me she was a sex worker. The woman would sit beside men for just a few rupee notes and give them a hand job. I froze when she stopped near my seat.

Trying to strike her best pose, the woman asked, 'Aiye hero, baithu kya god mein' (You want me to sit on your lap)? I didn't say anything and didn't move an inch. A man sitting a few seats ahead waved a ten-rupee note and she moved towards him. The woman took the seat next to him and sat with him till the interval. I decided that this much investigation was more than enough for one day. I hurried out in the interval.

Though I didn't see the full movie, I now had an idea of what the industry was all about and why it was flourishing. I was also amazed that people like me were still unaware of its more illegal components. I now had to find people who would give me the inside story.

Mad Hunt

I reached out to all the people in my circle who were even remotely associated with Bollywood. Everyone had a view on the flourishing C-grade industry. After a series of meetings, my search ended at a plush discotheque in the western suburbs of Mumbai which eventually turned out to be as shady as the theatres on Lamington Road.

It was the favourite haunt of most people in this industry. Even before you stepped into the pub, you knew you were not in the right place. It was a pick-up joint in the guise of a discotheque. As I walked to the door, I overheard snippets of conversations filled with filthy language. Once there, two hefty bouncers blocked my way. Since I was a new face, they refused to allow me inside without a female companion. I was asked to wait outside and give way to other people.

As I moved away, a girl in her mid-twenties followed me. She was dressed in a tight T-shirt that said 'They don't talk' in bold letters and jeans that were ripped in several places. 'Exkuj me,' she said, trying to force a weird accent, 'May I help to go in?'

I realized that she was a regular at the bar because as she led me inside, the bouncers and other staff at the gate gave her a broad smile and let both of us pass without any questions. She took me to one of the tables that was already half occupied and abandoned me there before vanishing.

I could see people from all walks of life on that dingy dance floor. The cheap fragrances and smell of gutkha were giving me a headache. The informer who had told me about this hangout had said, 'Har table par picture banti hai, sirji' (A movie is made at every table), and this was evident now. I could see the artists hovering around tables, talking to producers and directors. The group around me was also in talks about some script. But the producers were asking the artists to chip in with the money.

Suddenly the girl who had left me at the table arrived and sat down next to me. 'Kya karte hai aap (What do you do)? she said in Hindi. I told her I was a producer from north India and was looking for some artists to sign up for a movie. I told her that someone had told me about this pub and I had come to look for faces that I could launch. 'Will I get a role?' she asked with a smirk on her face.

I tried to convince her that I was looking for a different face and would require her as my assistant for the project. The woman accepted the offer instantly and promised to introduce me to some casting agents.

She identified herself by her nickname, Shabnam, and refused to reveal much about herself. But she gave me some incredible details on how this industry functioned. Shabnam had fled from her home town in Madhya Pradesh with a dream of becoming Kareena Kapoor, but after being used and abused she was pushed into the prostitution racket.

She had got a few roles in the beginning, but that was it. The casting agents had been exploiting girls for ages on the pretext of giving them roles. They were no less than pimps, she said. After talking to her for almost five hours, I realized that I could trust this girl. I told her, 'Look, I am not a producer. I am a journalist and I want to expose such casting agents. It won't be possible to catch hold of them unless people like you help me.'

I had judged incorrectly. The moment I revealed the truth to her, she got up and made to leave. Before she could inform the bouncers about my identity, I blocked her path. 'If you don't want to help that is okay with me but please don't create any ruckus here by informing the bouncers as I don't want to get beaten up,' I said. I gave her my card and briskly walked out of the pub.

There was no progress on the story for almost a week after that. But I was adamant on making it work. One afternoon, when I was leaving the office for an assignment, I received a call from an unknown number. 'Shabnam bol rahi hu' (This is Shabnam), the voice said. 'Bolo, Shabnam, mujhe pata tha tum phone karogi' (Tell me Shabnam, I knew that you would call),' I replied.

Shabnam was in need of some money to pay for the treatment of her teenage sister, who was suffering from a life-threatening disease. She asked me for Rs 10,000 that day. She said she would meet me the next day if I transferred money into her account. I decided to take a chance but after verifying a few things.

Through a friend who worked in the same bank where Shabnam had an account, I checked if the account actually belonged to her. Next, using her cell phone number, I requested a police officer who had been my friend for several years to verify her address too.

After I made sure of these two things, I transferred the money into her account and waited for her call. Shabnam kept her word. She called me again on the next day, 'Sahab, kaha milna hai' (Where do we meet?). We decided on meeting at the same pub.

'Sir, it's a huge industry. No matter what you do, it won't end. There are casting agents who are waiting for an opportunity to exploit the artists while many artists are waiting to offer themselves to such agents, producers and directors to get roles in their films. Girls are raped every day in this industry and no one cares about it,' she told me. I insisted that I still wanted to expose the horrors of this world.

She looked at me and said, 'Manoge nahi aap' (You won't give up). She said she would give me all the numbers the next day but reminded me that she could not accompany me for the story. I was relieved, as I did not want her to be in a dangerous position because of me.

The next day, Shabnam called me with all the required numbers. She kept insisting that I should chase a particular agent. I believed he was the one who had exploited her the most. With all the numbers in hand now, I had to have a strategy to lure them. Also, it was important for me to take someone along who could help me negotiate deals while talking to the actors. Being an outsider, it was not easy to talk in the industry lingo.

A friend who had once worked with a Bollywood actor agreed to help. The deal was that I would do most of the talking, but in case I got stuck, he would intervene.

We decided that my friend would pose as the director and I would be a producer at a made-up production house. We called a few agents and informed them that we were looking for fresh faces for a movie. We called two pairs of actors and actresses, too. One pair would enact the soft porn while the second one would act in the hardcore porn scenes, which would be inserted once the film was cleared by the censor board.

Following our conversation over the phone, two casting agents met us in a restaurant near Juhu. We recorded our first meeting on a hidden camera, which was affixed to my computer bag. The agents, who liked to be identified as coordinators, said they were Kamlesh and Ramesh. But we were quite sure these were their 'screen' names. They only gave us their first names and we also never bothered to ask their last names, fearing that it would arouse unnecessary suspicion. Impressed with our first meeting, the duo was convinced that we were genuine financiers. They agreed to work with us till we selected the artists of our choice and took an advance of Rs 2000.

After a chat that ran for over an hour, we told the duo that we were new to the industry and that our budget was low. We also informed them that we were yet to formulate our script, but they still had no questions. After two pegs of vodka, Ramesh said, 'Sir, script ka koi zarurat nahi hai. Aap paper pe scene likh ke doge toh bhi sab samajh jayenge,' (We don't need a script, even if you jot down the scene on paper we will make it happen), said Ramesh.

Echoing a similar opinion, Kamlesh added, 'You will have to make two copies of your film. One with soft porn to get clearance from the censor board. This print is usually sent to big cities while the second copy, which will have hardcore pornography footage, is sent to the smaller districts of northern India.' Kamlesh even said that he would introduce us to some of his distributor friends who would help us circulate copies to video parlours and smaller cinema halls. By the time they were an entire bottle of vodka down, the duo had given us a lot of incriminating input on the functioning, artists and the circulation of the industry. To keep ourselves sober, we had told our waiter to put very little alcohol and more soda in our glasses. After chatting for almost the entire night, the duo left in the early hours of the morning with the promise to see us later in the day. We invited these men to meet us at a hotel in (Andheri West), where we had taken a room for a couple of nights for the sting operation.

We were not very sure whether we could trust these men, but they kept their promise and visited us. They carried a huge album that had photographs of actors, each striking a different pose. All the artists had different prices, ranging from Rs 50,000 to Rs 2 lakh. The price tag included their fees to work for the film with an adjustment for 'compromise'. 'Compromise?' I asked one of the men. 'But we are not interested in sleeping with the artists,' I clarified.

'There is nothing to feel shy about, sir. It is part and parcel of this industry. Whenever an artist signs your film it is understood that she will compromise with you for your work,' Ramesh said.

Realizing that the two men had a lot of valuable information, we decided to tease out more details. We told them that we did not have a script or a title, but we were serious about investing in the film.

'Sir, aap tension mat lo, hum aapka saath denge jab tak aap phillam bana nahi lete' (Sir, you don't worry about anything, we will assist you till the film is made), Kamlesh said.

He then drew our attention to one woman in the album and said, 'Have a look at this artist, she is experienced. Her name is Parveen. She has worked in several C-grade films. She is available at the moment and you can meet her if you wish to.' The woman, who was posing as a banjaran in the photograph, was one of the popular stars of the industry. He claimed that she had worked with Shatrughan Sinha, Prem Chopra and other senior actors. I was stunned to know that Shatrughan Sinha had also worked in C-grade films and it showed on my face. Looking at my expression, Ramesh said, 'Sir, duplicate senior artists, I mean. Should I call her in the evening?'

Parveen was the same woman who had acted across the lookalike Shatrughan Sinha in the movie *Main Cabrewali*, which I had watched. We agreed to meet her. They also promised to get more artists by the evening. The men were very punctual and quick with their work. In less than three hours, they walked into our hotel room with Parveen.

C-grade Actors

The woman, who was in her late thirties, gave us a broad smile and shook hands with us. As she made herself comfortable on the single bed in our room, Ramesh said she had worked with several senior actors of the C-grade industry. She worked as an extra in Bollywood on a part-time basis, but the C-grade films were her bread and butter, Kamlesh told us. Looking towards Parveen, he said, 'Arey, tum bhi kuch bolo apne bare mein' (Why don't you say something about yourself).

Blushing slightly, Parveen added, 'I have been working for the past several years in films. I have got some CDs with me for your reference.' She removed a copy of her latest film, *Main Cabrewali*, and handed it over to me

'Phhamily ke saath mat dekhiyega' (Don't watch it with the family), she said with a smile. 'Zarur' (Sure), I replied.

Parveen then asked us about the scenes that would be required of her. Cutting her off halfway Ramesh said, 'Script is secondary. It is at a premature stage and is yet to be finalized. But there are two scenes in the movie. In the first scene, the woman will be shown naked under the shower.'

'The second scene, which will be inserted after the censor board clearance, will be a bed scene. It is a porn shoot in which the lead artists will be shown having sex,' intervened Kamlesh, winking at me.

This was enough for Parveen. She agreed to the terms without a single query. Her only condition was that the movie should release outside the city so that her family and relatives did not find out about it. We promised to abide by it and told Ramesh and Kamlesh that we were quite impressed with Parveen and that she would play the lead role for us.

'Thank you, sahib, thank you bherry much,' said Ramesh with a broad smile on his face.

But we also told them that they should line up some more artists, who would agree to sleep with us for a role. They readily agreed.

Since the meeting with Parveen continued till late into the evening, we decided to call it a day. My only worry now was that we had relied too much on this duo for our work, and if they failed to turn up with more actors on day two, we would end up paying an exorbitant amount for the hotel room that would exhaust our budget without any results. But so far, they had kept their word and provided no reason for mistrust. We gave them Rs 2,000 each and promised to pay more on day two.

The first time I began to have doubts about them was when they refused to pick up our calls the next day. Our calls either went unanswered or were disconnected abruptly. The friend who had accompanied me for the story said, 'They have conned us. We should not have paid them any money.' But I refused to agree with him.

We kept trying till almost four in the afternoon. Half of our day had been wasted. The only call we received was from the hotel reception to check whether we wanted to extend our stay as we were two hours past our checkout time. I had given up on the two men by now and started packing our belongings.

When I went to settle the bill, the staff pointed to a man who claimed he was waiting for me. 'This gentleman said that he knows you and that he wants to meet you in person. I asked him to wait at the reception since you were coming here,' said the receptionist.

'Sahib, Kamlesh ne bheja hai cashting ke liye' (Sir, Kamlesh has sent me for casting), the man said, pushing an album of portfolios towards me. Heaving a sigh of relief, I asked the receptionist to move the luggage back to our room and extend our stay. The man, who identified himself as Ajay, asked us to pick girls from the album he was carrying and assured us that he would get them to our room before the end of the day.

Kamlesh and Ramesh had proved to be resourceful again. Ajay showed us photographs of hundreds of girls across many albums, of which we chose fifteen women. Three of them turned up that evening for casting.

The same evening, a different pair of coordinators, also sent by Ramesh and Kamlesh, brought two other girls, Sharifa and Sonia, to our room. Both claimed to be senior actors in the industry. They were not part of the fifteen women we had requested for the role. After an informal introduction, the agents advised that we meet them separately. Sonia stayed back with the agent while Sharifa went out of the room and waited for her turn.

Introducing herself, Sonia claimed that she had been working in C-grade films for more than four years and had worked in at least a dozen movies. But she was not carrying any CDs to prove her claim. Once we were done with the introduction, Sonia told us that she would charge Rs 1 lakh as her fees. She even agreed to push the limits if the movie was released outside the city. Her second condition was that she would act under a pseudonym. Her casting agent whispered in our ear, 'Sir, iss amount mein compromije bhi ho jayega' (Sir, she would even compromise with you for the fees we pay). The whispers were loud enough to reach Sonia's ears. She looked at us and seemed to agree to the agent's claim.

She continued to chat with us for nearly three hours, giving us many details of the industry.

She promised to help us insert the uncensored scenes into the film with the help of her friends who worked as editors in some studios at Adarsh Nagar in Andheri.

Sonia was even ready to tell us the procedure to get the movie approved by the censor board.

Her information proved to us that every aspect of this industry worked in tandem.

It was Sharifa's turn after that. She entered the room with a mint in her mouth, trying hard to cover up the smell of gutkha.

After a formal introduction, she took a seat in front of us. Unlike Sonia, Sharifa turned out to be bold. As soon as I was introduced as the financier, Sharifa got up and sat close to me. On the pretext of showing me her profile, she tried to get too close for comfort and rub against my shoulder. The smell of gutkha was strong. I got up from my seat on the pretext of going to the washroom and my friend carried on the conversation.

Before we could make her an offer, she told us she would work with us for semi-porn videos. 'Jo bhi hai saaf saaf bata dena, mai kisi chij ko mana nahi karungi,' (Tell me everything clearly, I won't say no to anything) Sharifa said, hinting that she would agree to 'compromise' as well.

Though she looked very young and was childish in her manner of speaking, the girl sitting in front of me seemed to be much more experienced than Sonia or Parveen. She knew exactly how and when to play her cards. I couldn't help but notice that she had scars on her wrists. She probably harmed herself, a sign of the toll that the industry took on her and the treatment she must be facing.

'She is very open-minded. You can get things done your way if you sign her. She will charge around Rs 50,000,' her coorindator said. He had shown less interest in Sharifa than in Sonia because the latter's signing amount was almost double that of Sharifa's. It was obvious that he would get more of a cut from Sonia. We winded up the casting saying that we would give him a commitment only after meeting other actors.

After examining the footage, we realized we needed to meet at least one more girl who would work for us in hardcore pornographic scenes. The story would be incomplete without that aspect. I called up Ramesh and Kamlesh and praised them for lining up such wonderful actors. To win their confidence, I also told them that we had selected Parveen and Sharifa for the soft porn scenes and now we wanted two more artists for the hardcore porn scenes. They assured us that one artist would visit us that night. Yet again, they kept their promise.

Later that night, another coordinator, named Tiwari, entered our room with a plump woman who looked to be in her early twenties. She was wearing a black top and jeans and was accompanied by a middle-aged woman. My friend asked her to introduce herself. She said her name was Poonam. My friend asked, 'Lekin artist kaun hai' (Who is the artist)? 'Main hu, sir' (I am, sir), said Poonam with a smile.

The middle-aged woman was Poonam's mother. Tiwari informed us that Poonam would do the pornographic scenes in our movie and that she was available for a very cheap amount. 'Beta, ramp whaak karke dikhao' (Show them your ramp walk), Tiwari said, making space for her. I told him repeatedly, 'Tiwari, rehne do, bhai' (Let it be), but he insisted, saying that it was important for the producer and the financier to know the artists they were signing on.

Tiwari then asked her to walk between the two beds in the room. Poonam got up and wore her heels, which she had left at the door before entering the room. She started to walk from one end of the room to the other. She tried her best within the limited space, standing in front of us with one hand on her hips. My friend, who was sitting next to me on the bed in one corner of the room, folded his legs, fearing that Poonam would trip and fall over them.

She stood like that for almost five seconds. 'Okay?' she asked my friend, seeking his permission to stop walking.

'Bas ho gaya aaj ke liye' (This is enough for today), said my friend. While turning, Poonam flipped her long hair in my friend's face, trying to be playful with him. She even pretended to trip and landed on his lap. He looked at me and said, 'Dekhta kya hai, issko utha pehle' (Don't stare, lift her up).'

I asked Poonam to take a seat. Adjusting her clothes, she sat down and there was silence in the room for almost two minutes.

Trying to make conversation, I asked Poonam about her career and experience, to which she said that she had worked as a body double for various artists in Hindi and south Indian movies. Suddenly, Tiwari got up from his seat and asked Poonam's mother to wait outside the room. Tiwari told me that I could have a very frank conversation with Poonam. He even offered that I could see her strip to check out her figure, but for that I would have to pay Rs 5000.

I asked him to be considerate to which Tiwari said, referring to her profession, 'This is her roji roti, if she shies away from this she will die starving. At times, they are also accompanied by their father for the casting. The daughters are abused and raped in front of the fathers for roles in this industry. It is better not to talk about it further, please tell me if you wish to see her naked.'

When he realized that we wouldn't work with Poonam, he asked her to pack up and wait for him outside the room. When she was about to leave, I gave her Rs 500 for her transport from the hotel till her home in Nalasopara. I even parted with a few hundreds for Tiwari so that his mood would improve, but it hardly made any impact on him. He hurried out of the room with a long face, with less promising words to return the next day with some other girl. That was the end of our meeting.

I couldn't shake the depressing feelings after that. The plight of the parents who witnessed their daughters being abused and molested right in front of their eyes was beyond what I had imagined. We checked out of the room the same night.

The story was rolled out the next day in the 'Witness' segment on NDTV 24x7. It covered all the aspects of the industry, including the artists, directors and producers.

Soon after, many casting agents who had roamed fearlessly with the albums of artists fled the city. Since none of them had my contact number, they bothered my friend, accusing him of laying a trap for them. My friend in turn acted clueless and portrayed himself as the victim too.

Though the sting operation was done and dusted, it left a lasting impact on me. I was amazed not just at the industry that was flourishing but also by the kind of work women had to do to survive. This was an important story that people who live in denial about the reality of the glamour industry and the attitude towards sex in our country needed to know. As a journalist, all I could do was unravel such stories, one at a time. Some day, I hope these women get an opportunity to work with dignity.

SEVEN

Untold Story

I had never seen anyone look as distraught as the woman sitting across me. Her eyes were red and swollen, and she had been crying continuously for the last half an hour. 'I am a victim of sexual assault,' she had said as soon as we sat down in the visitor's lobby of the Times of India building.

She had arrived unannounced, demanding to meet me, in the middle of one of the busiest days—I was racing to file a story before the day's deadline. But before I could ask her to come back later, she launched into her story amidst sobs.

'He is a senior bureaucrat in Mantralaya—the administrative headquarters of the Maharashtra government.

I have been going there for some work. He has been demanding sexual favours from me every time I go to him,' she said, adjusting her dupatta. 'I am a lawyer. I read your newspaper every day and I know of the stings you do. Only you can expose this man,' she insisted.

I was shaken by the story. Rarely had I seen someone cry so much and with such anguish. As she continued to tell me more details, I knew that this would be a big story and probably even make it to the front page, if it was true. Also, the woman was in such a state that I couldn't leave her there. I wanted to help her and I knew I had to dig more. So, I began asking questions.

She immediately put forward one condition: that she would not reveal the name of the bureaucrat right away as he was extremely powerful and well known. She said that she would need a few more meetings with me before she could reveal her assaulter's name. She wanted to be convinced that this was the right way to expose the man.

She promised to call soon as she left. My mind raced, attempting to guess who the bureaucrat could be. I rushed back to my fourth-floor office, wondering when she would get in touch. I thought back to how she had praised the newspaper and the work I had done, feeling a certain sense of satisfaction.

A few days later, she came to my office again. This time, she appeared to be more composed. She stuck to her refusal to reveal the bureaucrat's name in the second meeting too. I tried to stay calm but was eager to know. She began narrating the story from four months ago, when she had visited Mantralaya to get clearance for a file. She said that at her very first meeting with the bureaucrat he asked for her personal contact number. Given that he was almost her father's age, the lawyer gave it unsuspectingly. A couple of days later, she started receiving messages wishing her good morning and good night, which she again ignored as harmless. But soon, the messages became more personal.

The file she had handed over to the bureaucrat had her address in the documents. One day, she was shocked to see him at her doorstep with a broad smile on his face. 'I was passing by. So I thought I would pop in,' he said.

Not knowing how to turn him away, she offered him a glass of water. She seated him in the living room and went to the kitchen to fetch water. When she turned around, the bureaucrat had walked up behind her and tried to touch her inappropriately.

'I screamed at the top of my voice,' she recalled. The bureaucrat ran out of the house, sensing trouble.

We needed evidence if we had to nail him. She said that despite her raising an alarm, the bureaucrat had not got the point. He continued to message her at odd hours. She had contemplated going to the police but then decided against it as the cops won't bother to touch a man who held such an important portfolio. The more I thought about this man, the more I was irked at the kind of liberty such men take. Who gives them power to harass women? What makes them think they can get away with anything and everything?

I decided to discuss the story with my crime editor, S. Hussain Zaidi. After I had told him the whole story, Hussain agreed to meet the lawyer with me the next day. On the third meeting, the three of us sat in the lobby, brainstorming on ways to nail the bureaucrat. The woman told us that he had called her last night, declaring that he would come to visit her two days later. This was it. It was too short a notice to arrange for the special cameras and recorders and conduct a thorough background check, but we decided to go ahead and lay a trap.

I then called up the woman and informed her that we would require a different room for the camera set-up, from where we would keep both of them in the frame. She agreed to arrange for another room, and we hired an entire team to execute the operation.

* * *

Over the next two days, the bureaucrat was in touch with the woman. He kept sending her messages that were meant to woo her. The night before his visit, the woman received a message saying that he would reach her place sometime the next afternoon. She informed us and we reached her place early that morning to ensure that the equipment was set up.

She offered us the flat next to her residence, which was empty; the owner had given her the keys. The technicians examined her flat and fixed the camera in an earthen pot that had money plant. Once the technicians had tested the equipment, we were ready.

The wait was nerve-racking. The bureaucrat had not been in touch for a few hours. Finally, her phone rang. It was him, informing her that he would reach in another ten minutes. Our crew hurried into the flat next door. The woman and I decided that if the man crossed his limits, I would call on her landline or in the worst scenario, ring the doorbell posing as a courier boy.

* * *

The room that I had occupied had a balcony from where the entrance to the building was easily visible. After five minutes, I saw a white Ambassador with a red beacon entering the compound. A police constable in uniform got out and opened the back door. I could hear my heart thumping as I observed his black polished shoes when he stepped out of the car. The woman had not revealed the man's identity till that point. Even when he emerged, I could only see his back, his Safari suit, grey hair and the wrinkled skin of his forearms. After waiting for a week, I was impatient to see his face. But I didn't want to peep out of the balcony and risk being spotted by the police guards. Without wasting more time, the man rushed into the building and I turned back towards the camera.

I finally saw his face when he entered the flat. Even a decade later, I can still picture it clearly in my mind. I could hardly believe it. He was indeed one of the most important bureaucrats in the government at that point. I feared what would happen if the operation went south, especially considering the important portfolio he held. But the risk had already been taken and there was no looking back.

The woman offered him a seat in the living room. When she went to the kitchen to fetch water, the man followed her. We couldn't see what happened as there was no camera set up in that room. Soon after, the man returned to the living room, followed by the woman. Thankfully, she had remembered our instructions that she should not be outside the camera frame for even a second and positioned herself accordingly.

After a brief chat over a cup of tea, the bureaucrat made his first move. He stood up from his seat and sat down next to the woman. He tried to put his hand on her shoulder and pull her towards him. The woman resisted and asked him to mind his behaviour. When he started getting more forceful, we called up on the landline. She stood up to take the call and went back to her seat, informing me in a hushed tone that everything was fine.

But that one call messed up everything. As she went back, the man sensed that something was off. He began scanning the room suspiciously. But luckily, he did not spot the camera hidden in the money plant pot. I could gauge from his body language that he was scared and anxious. Maybe he had overheard the woman talking to me over the phone. There was pin-drop silence in the room for almost a minute. Then he abruptly got up and said, 'I would like to take your leave now. I will drop in some other day.' I couldn't believe that all our effort was going to be wasted. It was a mistake to make that call, but I had been worried about the woman's safety.

The man hurried out of the flat and got into his car. I thought of how big the story could have been. I cursed my luck all of that week. All our effort and energy had been wasted in the last five minutes. I remembered how in one of the meetings with Hussain he had said that he would have loved to have his name on such a story.

But my disappointment lasted only for a few days. The woman called again. She informed me that the bureaucrat was visiting her that afternoon. 'I have asked him to stop coming home, but he is adamant,' she said.

We decided to take a second chance. I asked her whether we could use the same flat next door for the camera set-up, but she said it was impossible for her to arrange for it in such a short time. I called up the technician who had helped us the last time. Even he said he could not help me at such short notice. But he said that in case I could arrange for a television set and a VCR, he could give me some basic lessons on the set-up, which

I could then do myself. I was very grateful for his help but I first had to solve the problem of the space required for the equipment.

I went to the technician's house, which was hardly ten kilometres away from my own and tried to grasp as much as I could in one hour. I called up the woman and asked her to think of a place in her flat that we could use. There was no other option.

Once back home, I picked up the huge television set and loaded it into an auto. I also took the video cassette recorder with me. I still remember the puzzled look on my mother's face. 'Vechva jau chu' (I'm going to sell it), I told her with a wink.

She knew that I was kidding but her only concern was missing that day's episode of *Kyunki Saas Bhi Kabhi Bahu Thi*, the Indian soap opera popular at the time. Hurrying out of the house, I told her I would get the television back by evening.

Luckily I made it to the woman's house just in time. There I met another friend of hers, who was also an advocate. She claimed he had come to help set up the camera.

Since there was no extra space to keep the TV set and the VCR, I decided to keep them in the balcony adjoining the drawing room. Though it was very risky to be so close as even a little noise or movement could alert the man, it was the best available option as setting it up in the bedroom or kitchen was even riskier. I instructed the woman to block the door with a study table after I had set up and put lots of file and books on it to make it look like the balcony had not been accessed for a long time.

Meanwhile, I started looking for something in the house to which I could affix the camera. I found a stuffed toy gathering dust in a corner that I thought would be perfect. I made a hole in the centre, put my camera inside it and kept it on a wooden rack close by. The output of the camera was transmitted to the recorder and I could see the footage on my TV set. I placed two mics under the sofa where the bureaucrat would probably sit. With my fingers crossed, I switched on the TV and was relieved to find that everything was working. After my work was done, the door to the balcony was blocked with the table. The lawyer's friend had proved very helpful in setting up the equipment. He decided to join me in the balcony.

* * *

We waited for more than an hour. It was extremely hot outside but we could do nothing but bear it rather than risk going back in and being surprised by the bureaucrat's arrival. He was at such a position that he could easily get us arrested on false charges. In case something went wrong, we had no way to control the situation. We could not even think of calling the police as the cops would not dare touch him. There was no escape route either. We had decided that in case the situation got out of hand, we would call the woman on the landline from the balcony to deter the man from making any more moves.

After waiting for an hour-and-a-half, the bureaucrat reached the apartment with his convoy, which included two armed policemen.

I saw the man for the first time from up close. He wore a safari suit and black shoes with a flashy golden watch on his left wrist. He seemed to be very particular about his appearance or maybe he was dressed up for the woman. Not a single hair on his head was out of place and he had ensured that his moustache was trimmed, too. The wrinkles on his skin stood out more as he did not keep a beard.

The lawyer opened the door, and as soon as he entered the house, he put his arms around her. Despite repeated refusals, the man kept touching her shoulders again and again.

'Is this what you have come here for? I thought you wanted to talk about the files or some work,' she said. We had placed an audio device in the house and the two were clearly audible.

The bureaucrat was a little taken aback. He moved away and abruptly changed the topic. He went on to talk about how he was under tremendous pressure at the office. As the woman went into the kitchen to fetch some water for him, he followed her.

I was irked by the woman. I had given her clear instructions to avoid going to the kitchen or bedroom as we had set up only one camera. But soon after, she came back and sat down. The man followed her. I called on the landline number to alert her about her mistake.

'Madam, please try and avoid inner rooms. We don't have cameras there. It will ruin our operation,' I said.

'Okay, I will keep it in mind,' she answered and hung up.

'Who was it?' the bureaucrat asked, trying to read her face.

'It was a friend, she was confirming our meeting tomorrow,' she replied.

'She or he?' he asked, and started laughing at his own sad sense of humour.

In less than ten minutes, the man made another attempt to get close to the woman. He sat next to her and this time he pulled her towards him. She pushed him away. There was some conversation between the two but due to their movements, the mic moved, disrupting the audio. However, the video was still crystal clear and we could see the man getting more handsy.

He got up from the sofa and stood at a distance from the woman. He removed his clothes one by one. Displaying his orange underwear, he stood in front of the woman. I waited, unsure of what would happen now. The man pounced on the woman again while she pushed him and tried to kick him away. I thought I had enough evidence to nail him. I picked up my phone to call her on the landline, but surprisingly her friend asked me to wait. I was not comfortable with that.

Then the woman hurried inside the bedroom. I was shocked. How could she move out of the range of the camera, knowing that there would be no evidence of what the man was up to? I called on the landline to get her back in the frame but there was no answer. I almost stood up on my seat to peep inside the living room. 'What are you doing? Are you nuts? We both will get killed or arrested. Stop it,' her friend said.

'What kind of a friend are you? Don't you see your friend is at risk?' I shot back. Just as I was considering going in, the two came back into the frame. I couldn't believe what I saw. Instead of resisting the man, the woman was getting cozier with him. Moments later, I saw the woman playing with the man's genitals. This was unbelievable. I couldn't believe this was the same inconsolable woman who had visited me almost a month ago. The woman was semi-nude now, despite knowing that everything was being recorded. It was getting worse with every passing moment.

The woman lay on the sofa, while the man stood, touching himself. She helped him in the act and he masturbated on her. This time I could not control my anger and called her on her cell phone.

'What the hell are you doing? I am not here to record you having sex. Stop this now or I will walk out in front of him,' I said angrily.

Without saying a word she banged the phone. She hurried towards the naked man and asked him to leave the house because some relatives were dropping by. The bureaucrat got worried and quickly put on his clothes. He left the apartment as soon as he could.

As I saw his car leave the building gate, I barged into the living room. 'Are you out of your mind? Why have you called me here to record you getting intimate with him?'

The woman could not meet my eyes.

'What do you think you were doing? Will you please tell me?' I asked.

Trying hard to look into my eyes, she said, 'I was only trying to gather as much evidence as I could.'

But I didn't buy it. She knew how it would look on tape. Maybe she expected that I would edit those parts out. But the footage had become unusable the moment she had appeared as a willing participant. Even though the man had been inappropriate despite repeated attempts at being told not to do so, she had taken part in the end and that would not allow us to successfully pin down this man.

I was angry that the woman had used me as a pawn and been ready to flout the rules and go to any length to trap this man. The story never saw the light of day but it did help me be more discerning while conducting sting operations.

EIGHT

Sayed Zabiuddin Ansari, better known by his alias Abu Jundal, played a key role in the 2008 Mumbai terror attacks. The ten Lashkar-e-Taiba terrorists who unleashed violence and horror on the city would not have been able to execute their plans if they hadn't had someone guiding them on what to say, what to do and when to act. Born in a small village in Maharashtra, Ansari is thought to have become indoctrinated by the banned Students Islamic Movement of India (SIMI) after the Gujarat riots in 2002. He not only taught Hindi to the men who carried out the attacks but gave them detailed guidance on what to say when questioned and what message to propagate. But 2008 was not the only time he was involved in terror attacks. His involvement in the Kalupur station blast in Ahmedabad and the Aurangabad arms haul cases in 2006 are what first put him on the police's radar.

* * *

8 May 2006

Chinchwad–Manmad Highway

On 8 May 2006, the Mumbai unit of the Maharashtra Anti-Terrorism Squad (ATS) received a tip-off that a huge consignment of arms and explosives was on its way to Aurangabad from Nashik. The entire department was on high alert and top officers were chosen to be a part of a covert operation.

A team of about fifteen left Mumbai in three SUVs and each unit stationed itself at different spots on the Chinchwad–Manmad highway near Aurangabad. After several hours of waiting, the team waiting at Yeola, near Nashik, spotted a Tata Sumo. The vehicle had huge cartons on the back seat. When the officers waved to the driver to stop, he sped away, arousing their suspicions.

The team got into their car and began to chase the Sumo on the highway, as well as an Indica that seemed to be travelling with the Sumo. The team also alerted other officers about the location of the suspicious vehicle. After a long chase that went on for about seventy-five kilometres, the team managed to overtake the vehicles near Bhuvaneshwar temple in Khuldabad, close to Aurangabad, and arrested suspected terrorists Mohammed Aamir Shakeel Ahmed, Mohammed Juber Sayyed Anwar and Abdul Azeem Abdul Jameel Shaikh alias Raja. Zabiuddin Ansari is currently serving a life sentence in the same case.

The team recovered both the cars and seized 30 kg of RDX, 10 AK-47 rifles and 3200 rounds of ammunition in the raid. Jundal, who was in the Indica, managed to flee and was believed to have escaped to Pakistan.

Hailing from Beed district in Maharashtra, Jundal was on the radar of intelligence agencies which through phone intercepts traced him to Pakistan and got to know in 2012 of his plans to move to Saudi Arabia.

Jundal was picked up for questioning by the Saudi police in June 2012. A year later, Jundal was brought to India. He led the ATS to another hideout from where 13 kg of RDX, 1200 cartridges and 50 hand grenades were recovered. It was one of the ATS's biggest achievements since it was launched in 2007 in Maharashtra.

But this news was not what took Mumbai by storm. What shocked everyone was that a day before travelling to Aurangabad with the consignment, Jundal had taken shelter in a hostel meant for Maharashtra's Members of the Legislative Assembly (MLA) in Mumbai's Nariman Point area. The state legislature was abuzz with controversies as the Opposition levelled serious allegations against the legislator in whose room Jundal and his associate had stayed overnight. Following political pressure, a high-level probe was initiated to learn the truth. After six years of investigation, late home minister R.R. Patil in 2012 gave the legislator in question a clean chit citing that there was no record of the terrorists staying in his room. Here is the reason why.

A Week Later in Mumbai

While the probe was on, out of curiosity, I visited the majestic MLA hostel in Colaba to check how easy or difficult it would be to stay at the hostel. I expected the place to be heavily guarded but it was not; almost anyone could enter without any hassle. I waited opposite the hostel and watched people go in and out.

After waiting for almost half an hour, I tried to enter the premises, and as expected it turned out to be a cakewalk. I surveyed the entire building and examined some of the rooms that were open. I now had enough information about the entry, exit and building.

I got a table at a restaurant near the hostel and kept an eye on every customer entering, while sipping a cup of tea. I hoped someone would be able to help me live in the hostel. After some time, a man in a white kurta and pyjama entered the restaurant and sat across from me. He nodded when I asked if he stayed in the hostel. With a little prodding, he told me how he had got a room there.

He had come from Raigad to visit relatives in Mumbai but his friend who was supposed to arrange accommodation had not turned up. He then called up another friend who spoke to the MLA hostel's receptionist posing as a minister's personal assistant (PA) and got him a place to stay. I thought this was a superb idea that could work for me.

I went back to the hostel and spent the next few minutes trying to determine which MLAs had which room numbers allotted to them in the hostel through discussions with people. I decided I would try to enter room 307, which I had found belonged to Kupekar R. Desai, an MLA from Sangli.

This was my ticket to the hostel.

I went back to the office and by evening discussed the story idea with my editor Pankaj Upadhyaya. It was decided that I would make the hostel my home for the next couple of days. I would spend at least two nights and three days there, and at some point I would walk in with a girl to prove how easily accessible these hostels were despite being government buildings.

Check-in

I was prepared with a fake Sangli address, in case someone asked where I was from. Before checking into the hostel, I made a brief halt at a nearby hotel. It had a clear view of the hostel's entrance and the people entering and leaving the premises.

Then I went inside the hostel and sought the receptionist's help in locating room 307.

Conversation

Bhupen: I want to go to room 307. Have you got the key?

The receptionist searched for the key.

Receptionist: They [the occupants] have not surrendered the key. Why don't you call them?

Bhupen: Do you have any idea when they will be back?

Receptionist: I can't say anything about that room.

Bhupen: You don't know?

Receptionist: Sometimes they deposit the keys, sometimes they don't.

Bhupen: Any idea how many people are staying there?

Receptionist: Perhaps three.

Bhupen: Should I come back later?

Receptionist: Why don't you call them?

Bhupen: Is there a number to call?

She browsed through the register.

Receptionist: No number is registered. (Pointing to the entry in the register) A few people were staying in it. They moved out some days ago.

Bhupen: One of Kupekar's personal assistants has sent me.

Receptionist: Then call the assistant. He will tell you where the keys are. He will also know who is staying there right now.

Bhupen: How many rooms are registered in Kupekar sahib's name? 307 and 308?

Receptionist: No. Only 307.

I decided to take a chance and made my way upstairs to the third floor. Surprisingly, despite knowing that I did not have a key, the receptionist made no attempt to stop me. I was stunned that not a single person inquired where I was going. I saw people of all age groups and backgrounds, busy brushing their hair, ironing clothes or doing other chores.

A few months before I had decided to chase this story, a cop from the nearby Colaba police station had told me how this hostel was a big boon for youngsters pouring into the city from the remote districts of Maharashtra. Many of them would come to Mumbai in search of jobs and try to stay at these free guest houses by serving political parties in different ways. The hostel housed not just youngsters but also government officers visiting Mantralaya for various reasons. The police officer had added that though it was a great help to poor farmers and their children, the local authorities needed to have some security that restrained people from misusing the premises.

When I reached room 307, I found it was locked.

With no backup plan in place, I began to loiter on the floor, not knowing what to do. Rather than waiting for the occupants to return, I decided to look around for another room. I went to the second floor and located a room (204) that was not locked. I then made a few calls to a journalist friend and learnt that the room was registered in the name of Chandrashekhar Bhonsale, the MLA from Udgir, in Latur district. I called up a friend from the district and got a bona fide address to present in case I was questioned.

The room was hardly 400 square feet, with a single bed in one corner. The other corner had mattresses that were rolled up, indicating that the room was occupied by more than one person.

There was another room inside that was locked. The strong stench of gutkha and stale cigarette smoke made me feel sick. The thought of spending two nights in such a place gave me a headache. Trying not to focus on the filth, I leaned against the wall, which is when I spotted a big rat on the bedsheet eyeing me suspiciously. It jumped off the bed and scurried out of the room quickly. I left my bag and walked out to get some fresh air. After a stroll, I headed back to the hostel, consoling myself by repeating that it was a matter of just a few days.

My Roommates

Fifteen minutes later, a middle-aged man walked into the room. I nodded by way of saying hello. He responded similarly and identified himself as Sripat Kamble, a bus conductor from Udgir for the Maharashtra State Road Transport Corporation (MSRTC). I was reluctant to speak about myself but Kamble had his questions ready.

He didn't ask my name but inquired about my village. I was not able to give him a satisfactory answer and tried to put the issue to rest by telling him that I stayed very close to a sugar factory in Udgir. He asked me about some roads and villages nearby and seemed satisfied when I nodded in agreement a couple of times, but I did not want to take any chances and excused myself under the pretext of making a phone call.

On my return, Kamble pretended to be asleep on the only cot in the room, hinting that it was his place and I would have to sleep on the floor. I asked him about the other roommates.

He said there were a couple of youngsters and one Pawar, the PA to Bhonsale, in whose name the room was registered.

He said, 'Pawar sahib is inside.' I realized he meant behind the door that was locked. 'He must be praying now.' I was unnerved by the presence of the PA and left again on the pretext of going for a walk, leaving my bag in the room. I realized I could easily tell Pawar that I had been sent by another PA. I quickly called up some of my sources in Udgir and learnt the name of another PA.

I returned to the hostel about three hours later, at around 9.30 p.m. By that time, Pawar had left. There was another person in the room though, along with Kamble, calculating something. I went up to him and requested him to pass my bag that was lying next to him. But he replied rudely, 'Take it yourself, pal. I have just got back from duty. Don't bother me.'

I collected my bag, took out my tiffin and began eating.

A while later, the man came out and sat down in front of me. Kamble introduced me while the youth identified himself as Dilip Patil, an engineer working for a company in Lower Parel. Dilip asked where I worked, to which I replied that I was a photographer looking for a job. I told him that I would be staying in Mumbai for a couple of days as I had to give a couple of interviews. 'Stay as long as you want,' Kamble said in an authoritative tone as if he was the landlord. The two then warned me to take care of my bag as the place was prone to thefts.

After sheltering terrorists, this was a fresh charge against the hostel. I was told that there had been a series of thefts in the hostel but no one had bothered to approach the cops. The reason was that all the people living in the hostel belonged to poor families and had come to the hostel with bare necessities. Who would pursue complaints for such inexpensive things? They appreciated the opportunity to stay there. 'This is such lavish accommodation for villagers like us who have spent a major part of our lives in simple huts,' Kamble and Dilip said.

No Sleep at Night

After chatting with my roommates, I ventured out for some fresh air. Since that afternoon, I had entered and exited the hostel on several occasions without attracting any attention. It was worrying that the guards had not bothered to stop me even once. They had a logbook on a table in front of them where they were supposed to note details of the visitors but they happily chose not to do their jobs. Most of the time, I could see just one guard manning the desk while the other would either be walking about or taking a nap in one of the empty rooms.

At 11.30 p.m., the roommates began spreading mattresses on the floor to sleep. Thankfully, there was a mattress in the corner, and before anyone else could claim it, I laid my hands on it and spread it out close to the door.

As I was about to go to sleep, Kamble warned me that there were bed bugs in the mattresses. I thought he was pulling my leg and ignored him. I was more worried about the filth in the room and the claustrophobic atmosphere. Moreover, I was preoccupied with thoughts of uncovering more material for the story the next day.

In less than half an hour, I felt the bedbugs. They were all over my body. I battled for almost two hours but there were too many and I eventually surrendered. Out of sheer exhaustion, I finally fell asleep in the early hours of the morning.

I woke up soon after to the sound of a loud roar in the room. It was loud enough to wake up everyone in that tiny space except the person who was making the sound—Kamble. His snoring could be heard till the staircase leading to the other floors. Patil and his friends, who were also disturbed by the snoring, tried to shake Kamble awake, but to no avail. In fact, the volume of snoring only increased. They said, 'This man has not let us sleep for the last three days. God knows how many more days he is going to be here.' Eventually, they gave up and went back to bed. But I was unable to fall asleep after that.

Day Two

MLA hostels are often in the news for all the wrong reasons. In December 2003, a minor girl was raped by four boys inside the MLA hostel at Nariman Point. During investigations, the cops learnt that the girl was brought to Mumbai on the pretext of employment and eventually sold in the flesh trade market. She was forced to entertain customers in Mumbai's red light areas.

She was brought to the hostel by a pimp and was asked to entertain four boys who took turns to rape her. The cops received a tip-off about the incident and rescued her from there. The boys were booked on charges of rape and the subsequent investigations helped the cops bust the entire network.

I wanted to check if this incident had had any impact on the security at the hostel and whether it made any difference if a female entered the premises. After a quick shower, I had my tea and breakfast at one of the restaurants in Colaba and rushed to the office looking for a female reporter who would accompany me for the story. My colleague Hetal Vyas readily agreed to help. To look even more suspicious, I took a huge wooden carton in my arms. I thought that now the guards would find something amiss and stop me at the gate.

I reached the hostel with Hetal. Crossing my fingers, I began walking straight towards the staircase. I even tried to make eye contact with the guards, giving them enough opportunity to stop me. Unfortunately, nothing affected them. They were as good as wax statues placed at the entrance to welcome guests.

They allowed us easy entry, making it evident that the premises were not secure. We made no haste entering or exiting. Hetal and I strolled to my room without anyone intercepting us. Neither the guard nor the receptionist tried to stop us.

After spending almost three to four hours in the hostel, we walked out. I dropped Hetal back to the office and returned to the hostel.

Face-off with Pawar

When I came back, I saw Kamble lying on the bed in his favourite banyan and red shorts. After a few minutes, I tried to strike up a conversation and asked him if he had seen the other boys, to which he replied that he had no clue and went to sleep. A while later, I heard some noise from the inner room that was usually locked. I saw a shadow under the door. I disturbed Kamble once again and asked him whether he knew who was inside. 'It's Pawar sahib,' he said.

I was dreading confronting MLA Bhonsale's PA. I left the room again for a while, thinking that he would leave the place as he had done the day before. But several hours later, Pawar had still not left.

I gathered courage and made up my mind to face him. In case he called and cross-checked, I would mention the name of Bhonsale's other PA, which my journalist friend had told me.

As I reached the hostel, I saw Dilip packing his bag. He was leaving for Raigad to see a girl.

'Will you marry and bring your wife to the MLA's hostel?' I smiled and asked.

'I will buy a flat for her,' he said, snubbing me.

He bid farewell to Pawar, who was resting in his room. That's when Pawar came out of the room. I froze and tried to hide my face, pretending to be absorbed in checking emails on my phone. I could not look at him for even a second to know how he looked. But like all the security guards and other staff at the hostel, Pawar, too, did not seem to be bothered by my presence.

He handed Dilip Rs 100 to buy paan and a couple of cigarettes. He then looked straight into my eyes and ordered me to accompany Dilip for the cigarette run. I could not say no to him.

'This will be your responsibility till you stay here after I am gone. Since they provide us this place for accommodation, they want us to do these chores,' Dilip said on our way downstairs. He added that some PAs even asked roommates to wash their clothes, get them ironed, buy alcohol for them and at times give them massages in the evenings. I hoped I would have to do nothing of the sort on the last day of this operation. I came back to the room and handed over the paan and cigarettes. He asked me to keep them on the table and latch the door while leaving. I rushed out, fearing that he would ask for a massage.

I then spread my mattress and pretended to sleep. The second night was equally tough with the bed bugs and rats. But it was still better than massaging the MLA's PA. I was exhausted because I had not slept well in more than forty-eight hours. Lying on the mattress, I eagerly waited for the morning to wrap up the operation and go home.

Day Three

I now had enough information. On the final day of the operation, there was not much to do. By now, the guards and I were friendly enough to greet each other with a smile and even exchange a word or two.

Their dialect clearly revealed that they belonged to the remote districts of Maharashtra. It is always easiest and most helpful to strike up a conversation if you show interest in their home town. I asked them how long they had been deputed at the hostel. The guards told me that they had been working for the last couple of years and were tired of this posting. They agreed that they had less authority than a statue. When asked why they did not maintain records of visitors, the guards revealed that the PAs intervened every time they stopped people from entering the premises and questioned those who were accompanied by women.

'How do we perform our duties without any authority? Who wants to face the wrath of PAs who use filthy language? There is no option but to ignore our responsibilities,' said one of the guards. I understood their helplessness and felt a little less bitter towards their carelessness.

They told me how a month ago a paanwalla on the pavement had been injured by an empty bottle of alcohol thrown out of the window by an advocate staying on the third floor. Apart from that, thefts and robberies were rampant too.

Later, after I had left the hostel, I contacted the Joint Commissioner of Law and Order to ask about the major security lapses at the hostel and the allegations I had heard, including charges of rape against the people staying there and providing shelter to terrorists. He said that, on an average, more than a thousand people entered the hostel weekly and not everyone could be checked by the guard. That is the only response I received to explain the lack of security I had witnessed. None of my credentials or documents had been checked while I was there.

The cops said they had requested the hostel management to increase security several times but in vain. Officials of the Public Works Department (PWD) did not reply to calls and made no attempt to justify their actions. However, two days after *Mumbai Mirror* carried an exposé on the lax security, the government introduced a system of issuing identity cards to all visitors across the four MLA hostels in the city.

Following the report, the former principal secretary of the Maharashtra Assembly, A.N. Kalse, dashed off a letter to then superintendent of engineers of the PWD, A.B. Gaikwad. The letter stated that every visitor to the city's MLA hostels would be given identity cards and their personal details be registered in a logbook only after they provided an authority letter from an MLA. The PWD and the police officials also started making constant rounds of the hostels. But a foolproof security system was still lacking.

Such revelations made a great story for Bhupen Patel, the investigative journalist, but were bad news for Bhupen Patel, a resident of Mumbai, and one of the many who never fall out of love with the city's vibrancy, undying spirit and magnanimity. I was heartbroken every time I or fellow journalists broke such stories.

The least people in power can do is not leave the city, which gives them their power, shelter and bread, vulnerable to such abuse. With the hope that it would make a difference some day, I remained driven to keep exposing such situations.

NINE

While Indians may largely remember the 1990s for the Bollywood music of the time, the police officers of Mumbai will largely recall the Internet revolution that stormed the country, primarily the metro cities. Internet addiction was at its peak by the late 1990s, when the younger generation got access to the world wide web. Video game parlours were now a thing of the past, and cybercafés provided access to not just games but also pornography and all kinds of websites. Owners were happy to make a fortune from the people lining up to surf the Internet; many cafés even offered small cubicles to ensure privacy.

Some youngsters with a different kind of curiosity ended up using the Internet for purposes that became one of the biggest concerns for the police. These people wanted to be 'disrupters' to prove their supremacy over the lawmakers and law enforcers.

Hacking, which is common now, had just started emerging as a crime. Gradually, the cases were too many and the expertise of the local police stations too limited to deal with it. This is when the Mumbai Police decided to set up a special cell that would deal only with cybercrimes.

Some of the most tech-savvy cops from the Computer Cell were selected to be part of the new unit. They were trained under the guidance of cyber guru, the late Vijay Mukhi. Mukhi taught them about the strengths and weaknesses of the medium and prepared them in case a high-tech case was referred for investigation. The unit also outsourced work to experts.

It was 2001. I had spent just two or three years in the field of journalism, working as a reporter at *Mid-Day*. I was trying hard to develop a network of sources to leave my mark on the industry, and my hunger for good stories always kept me on my toes.

* * *

In early June 2001, I started receiving anonymous calls from someone who sounded like he could not be more twenty-two years old. He never told me his name and every call was to inform me about his hacking achievements. Sometimes he would say he had hacked websites in other countries or institutions to show how vulnerable they were to cyberattacks. I could tell he was passionate about establishing himself in the digital world the way I wanted to make it big in journalism, and I felt a strange sense of connection to him.

Though none of this was printable, I nurtured him as a source, anticipating that he would be useful to me some day. Neither of us insisted on meeting each other, but we kept in touch over the phone and at times discussed his motives for hacking.

But what brought us closer was something beyond my wildest imagination. One evening, a call on my office landline became a turning point for my career. It was him. But his voice sounded different. There was a mix of excitement, fear and anxiety in his tone, and it was obvious that he had done something big. 'I hacked the Mumbai Police's website,' he said. Now I was scared because I could possibly be considered an accomplice. I said, 'Abey, bahut marenge tereko, tu ghar pe bola kya' (They will beat the hell out of you. Did you tell your family)? I had hoped he was kidding, but he replied, 'You think this is a joke? I am very serious. Go to their website and you will see that their homepage is disrupted.'

I immediately logged in and saw that the homepages of two sites—cybercellmumbaicity.com and www.ccicmumbai.com—displayed the Information Technology Act and other laws pertaining to IT Act violations. He wanted to call out the cops for letting their guard down.

The young ambitious journalist and the idealistic young citizen in me were in a tussle. This would be my biggest scoop till date if I reported it. I was torn between writing about it and reporting it to the police. He probably sensed my indecisiveness because he hung up saying he would call back in fifteen minutes.

I rushed to my editor's cabin and discussed the story with him. We decided to persuade the caller to meet and I would record the interaction on a phone camera. I would also carry a pen camera as I anticipated that he wouldn't let me take his picture. We would take a call later on whether to identify him or not.

I went back to my seat and waited for his call; I wasn't sure if he would call me back. But exactly fifteen minutes later, the phone rang again. This time, he sounded more confident. I made my request to meet him, but he hung up, thinking that it was a set-up for the cops. Before he could cut the call, I managed to tell him, 'I am as hungry for this story as you are for glory in the cyber world, so please have faith in me and give me an opportunity to meet you once.' But he did not give in.

I lost my cool and banged the phone down, startling the entire office. 'What's wrong with you?' a colleague sitting next to me asked in an irritated tone. I preferred to ignore her and walked out for a break.

I had never anticipated that I would lose the story so easily. At that time, it felt like I had lost the one opportunity to kick-start my career. I was most upset that I had not been able to convince him.

When I returned, a colleague told me that someone had called and left a message that he would call back again in a few minutes. 'Did you ask his name?' I asked. The caller had just replied saying that it was an important call. I heaved a sigh of relief. It had to be him. And I was right. The hacker called me back.

'I am talking to you only on one condition. You will not mention my name. I want you to come alone near Kabutar Khana in Dadar. I will see you in exactly one hour,' he said, referring to the pigeon-feeding square in Mumbai's central neighbourhood.

'But how do I recognize you? Can I have your number?' I asked.

'Once you reach the spot, I will give you a call and give you further instructions,' was his reply.

It seemed like he had learnt his moves from films. I informed the office and rushed to Dadar without wasting any time. It took me less than half an hour to reach the spot. I kept looking at the people passing by and saw him in every young boy that walked past me; I even tried to make eye contact with some. Exactly an hour after the last conversation, I got a call on my mobile number from a landline number. From where I stood, I could see three public call office (PCO) booths, of which two were busy. One was occupied by a middle-aged man while the other had a younger boy. I was sure the latter was the one I was looking for. The hacker asked me what I was wearing. On hearing my response, he cut the call. The young boy also put down the phone. The boy then began walking straight in my direction. As I raised my hand in greeting, someone tapped me on my back and said, 'I am the one you are looking for.'

I turned around and saw a six-foot-tall plump boy standing behind me. He was wearing a green T-shirt with beige three-fourth pants. He kept looking around shiftily to make sure there were no cops nearby. I assured him and asked him to relax. 'Let's go to a more secluded place and talk, this spot is not safe,' he said and led me towards one of the smaller lanes in Dadar.

He still refused to tell me his name. 'I am going to be Dr Neurkar for you, you don't have to know my real name. Let's keep it that way,' he said. I learnt later that his pseudonym was inspired by Dr Neurkar of G-Force, the world-renowned hacker.

Though he was extra cautious about scanning our surroundings for danger, he missed the pen camera in my shirt pocket. At that time, the pen camera was not very common.

Once we sat down outside a shuttered shop, he revealed a few more details about himself, telling me his larger circle of friends was also responsible for hacking the Mumbai Police's website.

'And your motive?' I asked him.

'What kind of training are these officers getting when they cannot protect their own online properties? How will they protect the sites of others? Only passing the Indian Police Service exams is not enough for these guys, they should also be aware how to prevent cybercrimes in Mumbai. They must keep up with the times. The agency that is fighting for justice for the victims of cybercrime has to first secure itself,' he explained.

'If you notice the trends in the US and European countries, crimes on the Internet are far more complicated. We only want them to take this as a lesson,' he said, as if he was doing some kind of service to the police department.

The hacker said that he was part of a thirteen-member team called G-Force. Other members on the team were Da Libran, Lil_dvil and The_anaylizer, all of whom were Indians. Seven of the members were Pakistani nationals while the remaining two were Russian. All members were in constant touch with each other over the Internet and worked as security advisers to companies abroad.

'Have you considered sharing this with the police?' I asked.

He snubbed me and said, 'Do you think they would agree that the team that is manning one of the first cybercrime cells in the country is incapable of handling the cases? They would never do that,' he added.

'Any fear of consequences?' I asked.

'I have to take this gamble. If the police force is sporting enough to take criticism and improve their ability to deal with what is anticipated in the future, it will benefit the city,' he said.

After chatting for almost two hours, the hacker sensed that I could be trusted. He agreed to get in touch in the next two or three days. But the deal was that he would call on my landline and start with the secret code: 'Dr Neurkar of G-Force'. Gauging that he was comfortable talking to me, I requested him to give me a photograph of himself without revealing his identity. Though he refused flatly initially, he agreed after I persisted. He allowed me to take a picture where his back was to the camera. 'Boss, I am taking a big risk trusting you. I hope you will not break my trust,' he added. He was still unaware that our entire conversation was being recorded.

I was in two minds now. The innocence I had seen in his eyes made me feel guilty about exposing his identity, but my newspaper had given me clear instructions to get him on tape. Sometimes my profession demands things that the heart doesn't support. I reached office and sat at my desk. It was now very close to the deadline and my editors worked with me to figure out how to position the story.

They bombarded me with questions. 'How did the interview go?' 'Who is this man?' 'How old is he?' Had I managed to catch him on camera? I connected my pen camera to the computer to view the footage. Strangely, the video had not been recorded due to a technical snag, but I still had an audio recording.

My editor yelled at the top of his voice when he found out what had happened. 'Useless, ch****a, g****u! You missed the golden chance. What is the point of running the story now? We don't have a face for the man who is throwing a challenge to the cops to come and arrest him,' he said.

The pressure was mounting as the deadline approached. I thought I would lose my job soon after beginning my career.

After a minute of pin-drop silence, I gathered courage and told my city editor, Lajwanti D'Souza, that I had a photograph of the man's back.

'Okay, let me talk to him (editor) and figure things out,' she said and walked into the editor's cabin. After a brief chat, she came out and hurried towards me. We would carry the story with the photograph. When I called the cops for their side of the story, they maintained that their in-house hackers had penetrated the site for an experiment. This did not explain the changed homepage, a classic hacker trademark. The police also claimed that the hacking was over, but the site hadn't been fully restored till early next morning.

When the story broke, it was everywhere. Every newspaper had reported the news about the police website being hacked, but we outshone the others with the interview of the hacker. I still remember that a senior reporter from a rival newspaper who I could barely stand approached me to offer his congratulations. However, he tried to mask it by talking about the layout of the story and not the content.

In just a few hours of the issue reaching the newspaper stands, I was chased by almost every news channel and multiple police officers who wanted to know where they could find the hacker. I received close to a hundred calls, inquiring whether I would share the number of the hacker.

Senior officers of the Crime Branch, who usually made me wait outside their cabins for hours for one quote, called up and requested that I visit them for tea. A deputy commissioner of police, who I had known for a while, wanted the hacker to surrender and asked me to convey the message to him. But I was firm. I had betrayed the hacker enough and could not expose him any further. He had not wanted publicity. His 'social service' was highly misunderstood by the police, as he had anticipated.

The cops were under tremendous pressure to trace the guy. The Cyber Cell traced the hacking to an Internet café in Dadar. They arrested the owner, Pradeep Yadav, and a hardware engineer, Jagdish Sabnis, who had no clue about the hacking. In those days, the cafés maintained no records of visitors, making it more difficult for cops. The city also had no CCTV surveillance. I was sure the cops would have no option but to tap my personal numbers. After a while, I decided to use only the office landline phones as it is difficult to receive permission to tap landlines of newspaper organizations.

Soon after the story was published, I was advised by my office legal team to stop communicating with the hacker. Almost a week after the story broke, the hacker called me on the landline. 'Dr Neurkar of G-Force. The two arrested have nothing to do with the case, they have been framed,' he said.

The police had claimed that they had concrete evidence against the duo and that one of the accused had already confessed. The two arrested were detained under various sections of the Information Technology Act and several sections of the Indian Penal Code. They faced a minimum sentence of three years.

'I called the senior police inspector of the Cyber Crime Cell, I.M. Zahid,' the hacker continued.

'Why would you do that?' I asked.

'I asked him, "Pakad rahe ho ya nahin" (Are you going to arrest me or not)?' he replied.

'What! Are you out of your mind?' I said.

He gave me Zahid's cell phone number as proof and then abruptly disconnected our call. We published another story about him, claiming that he had mocked the cops about arresting him. The day the story was published, the pressure on the cops increased. It turned out that this call would set off Neurkar's downfall. He had dared to do something that even hardcore criminals and gangsters would not think of doing.

In a closed-door meeting, the then joint commissioner of police, Bhujangrao Mohite, involved other units of the Crime Branch in tracing this man. This meant that almost half a dozen police units were desperately looking for him. The officers were instructed to find him in a week's time. It was a matter of prestige and every officer in the unit wanted to be the one to solve the case.

Three computer experts, part of the Mumbai Police's advisory committee, were also called in: Internet guru Vijay Mukhi, and ethical hackers.

In less than a week, the Crime Branch cracked the case and arrested Anand Ashok Khare, then 23, alias Dr Neurkar and Mahesh Subhash Mhatre, also 23, alias Da Libran. Khare had dropped out of a telecom engineering programme and was a Cisco-certified network associate, while Mhatre was a software programmer.

The officers involved in the operation were extremely proud. The Crime Branch called a massive press conference to share the details of the case. At the conference, the officials said that several attempts had been made to hack the police's site from two particular internet protocol (IP) addresses in July. Both belonged to cybercafés in Dadar, one of which was run by Mhatre.

Meanwhile, following Dr Neurkar's digital tracks left behind on computers in Mhatre's Nexus Cyber Café, authorities honed in on a single computer. Crime Branch officers interrogated the cybercafé staff and nearby restaurants and came up with the rough sketch of a youth who lived in the neighbourhood and surfed the web till early in the morning. The next morning, police arrested Khare from his house in a three-storeyed chawl near the congested Dadar railway station. The stockily built six-footer broke down and admitted to being Dr Neurkar. Mhatre had been his accomplice, Da Libran.

Another explanation for Khare's arrest was his website, maharaja.webjump.com, which had a passport-size photograph of Khare and a promise to teach surfers how to hack. 'We hack, we teach, we make history, we are the analysers,' it proclaimed. His penchant for publicity had also helped the police trace him. The cops claimed that they had matched the photograph in the paper with the one on his website for final confirmation.

The authorities were determined to have this man in jail for a long time. Though Khare and his friends got out on bail after three months, they were charged with credit card fraud soon after based on frivolous evidence.

In one of Khare's interviews to a newspaper after his release post the credit card case, he alleged that the police had waited till he got bail before filing the second case. He said, 'They suspect that I am involved in some credit card fraud and had used an e-mail address of sycho6598 to hack into some system because my phone number ends with 659. Now if I was the hacker with 225 credit card numbers in my possession, I would have been a rich man. I would have robbed the money and escaped from India but like other poor people I live in a chawl.' He also complained about the treatment the police had given him. He said they hit him on his feet, abused him and forced confessions.[2]

Since Khare had not given me any number, we were not in touch for eight to nine months. My legal team in office also suggested that I stay away from him as it

---

[2] Times of India, 3 September 2001 (online).

would invite legal complications. But I wanted to see him after his arrest to understand what was going on in his mind.

One evening when I was returning to Dadar station after an assignment, I heard someone call out my name from the far end of Kabutar Khana. It was him. I had not expected to bump into him again.

'Kaisa hai' (How are you)? I asked.

'I am okay, hope you too are doing well,' he said.

We decided to sit at a coffee shop nearby. I asked, 'What's up?'

'Bahut mara mereko, yaar, tyre mein daal ke mara. [I was brutally beaten up by the cops. They hung me in a car tyre and beat me.] They were forcing me to say things but I refused. It would also have invited trouble for you, brother,' he said.

He told me that Mhatre had even filed a case with the State Human Rights Commission about the way the police had treated him.

After that meeting, Khare remained in touch with me and the cops for months. While his case was being heard in the court, the Crime Branch officials worked with him to trace hawala transactions of underworld gangs. He even helped them uncover a big money trail that led to the underworld don Chhota Shakeel.

Despite his extraordinary skills, Khare found it difficult to get a job. During one of our conversations, he told me that one of the companies to which he had applied as an e-security consultant had sent him a letter stating, 'Your name is greater than ours in the industry, so kindly excuse us.'

But this had not discouraged Khare from helping the cops or even staying in touch with me. There was something very endearing about him. He held no grudge against me for running the article. He is a source I will never forget and I will always question my decision of recording him surreptitiously. Even the police department grew fond of him. His bond with them grew so deep that they helped him find a job so that he could leave his past behind and start a new life.

TEN

July 2007

The assistant commissioner of police (ACP) of the Agripada division in Mumbai received a call. It was one of his regular informants who told him that a certain don, who was currently serving a sentence in a murder case, had asked to be taken to the emergency ward of a government hospital due to severe pain in his abdomen. His request had been granted but what was suspicious was that the caller had seen a woman accompanying this man.

The ACP rushed to the hospital and demanded to be taken to the prisoner's room. The on-duty doctor tried to stop him at the entrance. Enraged, the ACP slapped the doctor; it echoed in the corridors and almost everyone on the floor froze.

When the ACP finally entered, he found the don in a compromising position with the woman. It turned out that this wasn't the first time this had happened. When he interrogated the hospital staff, the ACP found out that the don did so regularly with the blessing of doctors.

He used to visit the hospital once a month to have sex with different women. His gang members would make all the arrangements. The doctors guarded the premises to ensure that the don was not disturbed for at least three hours and were rewarded handsomely in return.

But a case was never filed in the police station as the doctor clung to the ACP's feet and refused to budge till he agreed not to register an offence against him.

Most high-profile arrests in India have resulted in the convicted trying to avoid going to jail under the pretence of being admitted to hospital. The right to medical treatment for prisoners and undertrials has been blatantly misused in the country for ages.

Several politicians, high-profile businessmen and underworld dons are protected by doctors in the name of medical treatment. Though such reports have been the subject of several headlines and many inquiries have been made to investigate the role of doctors in helping the accused, not a single doctor has been found guilty till date. Under the guise of ill health, the accused are able to procure anticipatory bail in court while those convicted and in jail are able to take a break from prison life.

* * *

Five Months Later

When I heard of this instance, it remained with me and pushed me to expose such rampant abuse of power. I decided to visit J.J. Hospital in Byculla, where I saw prisoners being brought from Arthur Road Jail, Mumbai's main prison, for medical treatment and meetings with their family. I posed as the brother of a convict lodged in the jail and got talking with a person waiting in the crowd.

I found out that the setting happens at the jail. The prisoners would pay the in-house doctors, who would then refer them to J.J. Hospital for a temporary break. The break not only helped the criminals live comfortably, but also helped them coordinate with their gang members. In the past, several cases have been registered against convicts and gangsters for conducting business in the prison wards of government hospitals.

According to the man I met, convincing the doctors in prison was a cakewalk provided the prisoner had money. Those who couldn't afford to pay were denied hospital visits unless they were critically ill. Once the patient reached J.J. Hospital, the ward boys would mediate on behalf of the doctors and strike a deal with the prisoners for the amount they would have to pay to stay in the hospital. The money depended on the number of days the prisoner wanted to spend in the hospital. I found out that doctors not only helped people in jail but also gave authentic medical certificates to people who wanted anticipatory bail.

I thought of how I would expose this racket. Getting a prisoner to help catch the doctors red-handed would be next to impossible and hence I decided to gather evidence through a second option. I began working on a plan.

After a discussion and brainstorming session in the office, we decided to dig more into the story. One of my female colleagues, Priti Gupta, would accompany me for the story, posing as my sister. She would approach the doctors on the pretext of admitting her brother, Bhupen Shah, who was on the cops' radar for a cheating case.

At the hospital, we saw several patients and their relatives from across the state waiting for admission. As one of the biggest government hospitals in Mumbai, there was a lot of pressure on this medical centre. Many patients were heard complaining of ill-treatment by doctors and said they had been left unattended for days. Till a few years ago, before the hospital's administration was changed, the ward boys ran a notorious network. More than the doctors, it was they who decided a patient's date of admission and discharge by collecting money from the patient's relatives.

Their network was so deep-rooted that as soon as someone stepped into the hospital with an exceptional request, they would be approached by the ward boys.

After surveying the premises and making a few casual inquiries, we started looking for ward boys who we thought would be of use in a sting operation.

Priti approached a ward boy and told him that she wanted to admit her brother to the hospital. When he told her to talk to the chief medical officer (CMO), she told him the matter wasn't so simple. She then went on to recount how her brother, Bhupen Shah, had a case registered against him at the Malad police station and could be picked up by the cops any time. She stressed how we wanted admission so that I could apply for anticipatory bail. The ward boy still directed Priti to the on-duty CMO.

When we approached the CMO, he asked for Priti's cell phone number, called up somebody and gave that person her number. From his tone, we gauged that the CMO was wasting our time and had no clue of who could help us. We left the ward dead tired and disappointed, thinking that we would have to revisit the hospital the next day. It looked like it would be tough to infiltrate this network.

While we were sitting on a bench with relatives of other patients, Priti received a call from an unknown number. The person on the other end identified himself as Vijay More and asked her to meet one Yeshwant Dalvi outside the hospital gate. This was our first lead.

We met the man outside the gate. He was dressed in a white pant and shirt and asked Priti to explain the problem. Dalvi heard the entire story without interrupting. From his expression, it was evident that the man was convinced that our case was genuine. At the end he said, 'Aap tension mat lo, mai aapko phone karega raat mein, pehle main doctor se baat karta hu' (You don't worry. I will call you in the night after speaking with the doctor). The meeting had lasted almost one and a half hours. On inquiries with the hospital staff we learnt that Dalvi was working in the hospital's orthopaedic department.

At 8 p.m., he called and said he had spoken to the doctor. I would be admitted the next morning if we paid Rs 1.5 lakh as bribe. Dalvi made it clear that he was asking for the money on the doctor's behalf and admission would happen 'as soon as the money is paid'. He also gave us details of the admission procedure.

Since we had a budget constraint, the office asked us to negotiate and reduce the amount as much as possible. But we refrained from negotiations in the beginning, fearing that it would put him off. We kept him engaged to give the impression we were genuinely looking for help.

The next day, we visited the hospital again, hoping to try in person to negotiate the bribe amount. We had mentioned it over the phone to prepare him.

Conversation between Priti and Dalvi[3]

Priti: Are you sure my work will be done?

Dalvi: 100 per cent. I have spoken to my doctor. You just get the full amount. And ask Bhupen to mention back pain as the reason for getting admitted.

---

[3] https://mumbaimirror.indiatimes.com/mumbai/cover-story/to-avoid-jail-pay-rs-1-25-lakh-and-get-hospitalised/articleshow/15778119.cms.

Priti: If the doctor knows, why does my brother have to talk of back pain?

Dalvi: Just to show the junior doctors. They should not get suspicious about you or my sahib.

Priti: But Rs 1.5 lakh is too much. Can't the amount be reduced?

Dalvi: No, no. I've already told the doctor you're from a middle-class family. Normally we charge Rs 3–4 lakh in such cases.

Priti: How do I have to pay?

Dalvi: Full payment. We don't take part payment.

Priti: You're sure we won't have any problem once the amount is paid?

Dalvi: Not at all. Don't worry. Everything will be done according to procedure. Bhupen will get a discharge card after he is discharged, and if required, the doctor will also come to court to explain the kind of treatment your brother was given.

After this conversation, Priti and I headed for the hospital and reached around 2.30 p.m. More, the man who put us in touch with Dalvi, met us first on the premises and we carried on negotiations while we waited for Dalvi, who said he'd join them on the ground floor soon.

Priti: Please ask Dalvi to reduce the amount.

More: I can't do anything as the money part is handled by him and his boss. Dalvi has been in J.J. for twenty years and he is very close to the doctor. Admitting a person who has a case against him is not new in this hospital. It's done in the orthopaedic and general medicine departments.

Bhupen: What if I get arrested before I'm admitted? And what if I'm sent to jail? Will I be able to manage bail even then?

More: If that happens, you just manage the jail doctor. Once you come here, we'll take care of you, though it is difficult. The main man is Dalvi, he has access to a lot of doctors.

Finally, Dalvi joined us.

Dalvi: Have you got the money? I have spoken to the doctor (pointing his finger towards one of the doctors, who was leaving the hospital). He is just sitting in his car. He has already instructed his junior to take care of your case.

Priti: Can't we meet the doctor? If we are giving so much money, we should at least know who the doctor is.

Bhupen: We have some queries. I am a bit scared to get into this.

Dalvi: Your case papers are ready. Once you are admitted, your file will be ready. But you need to make the full payment. You will be admitted for back pain for a week.

Bhupen: But we cannot give you full payment. We are almost bankrupt, please reduce the amount. The case against me isn't so big.

Dalvi: Impossible. You have to trust us, we'll get you admitted. We have handled bigger cases. People come from as far away as Uttar Pradesh and Punjab. Sometime ago, I admitted a man from Punjab involved in a drug case. A huge amount had to be paid to get him admitted. We're not asking much from you. We take Rs 4–5 lakh from other people, but you are like my younger sister (addressing Priti).

After three hours of negotiations, we left as Dalvi and More refused to bring the price down. We continued negotiations over the phone till late evening. They told us that if I was not admitted immediately, we'd have to wait two more days as the doctor would not be on duty for the next forty-eight hours. We said we'd come to the hospital the next morning with the money.

We reached the hospital early on 16 January, and met Dalvi outside the OPD ward. Here we renegotiated the amount, and Dalvi finally agreed on a sum of Rs 1.25 lakh.

Dalvi: Have you got the money?

Priti: Not the full amount, but someone will be here in a few hours with the entire amount. You start the admission procedure.

Dalvi: Admission will just take half an hour, but you must get the full amount. You wait here, I will come in some time.

We then called More on his phone.

More: Again you have come without the money? What's the point? We will not be able to do it. Dalvi and his boss will get angry. You deposit the full amount and he will get your brother admitted.

Priti: I promise you the full amount is ready, it will reach us in some time.

Bhupen: Please do it for us, the cops came again this morning. I have Rs 15,000 with me; if I go back, they will arrest me.

More: Okay, let me speak to Dalvi.

We were then told to wait for Dalvi, but when he didn't turn up for two hours, we approached the ward boys. One of them told us that a ward boy from the OPD might be able to help us. He was right, as the ward boy outside the OPD led us to the doctor's cabin and asked us our problem. He was keen to know the details of the case I was involved in. Luckily, I remembered a case about an embroidery factory owner I had reported on in the past and used that to concoct my own story. The ward boy promised our work would be done if we were ready to give the money to the doctor. We were then directed to the registration counter to provide the case papers. Dalvi, meanwhile, got to know through his network that we had approached another ward boy. He came to the counter and led us to another doctor's cabin and asked us to wait outside. The doctor was in by now and Dalvi went in to meet him. Minutes later, we were asked to enter.

I repeated the same story to the doctor.

Doctor: What is your name? What do you do?

Bhupen: I have a small embroidery business. The final product is sent to Dubai. I took a contract from a man who gave me work but did not come to collect his consignment for a long time. Finally, I sold the material to some other party. After a while, the party to whom the consignment belonged approached me and registered a complaint with the police.

Doctor: Are you telling the truth?

Bhupen: Yes, doctor.

Doctor: Only then can I help you. Where are you from, Orissa or Gujarat?

Bhupen: Gujarat.

The doctor then jotted down something about chest pain on the medical papers.

Doctor: Whenever any doctor comes to you for a check-up, just say you have chest pain.

He called in his junior and briefed him on my case.

Doctor: You take care of him, he has chest pain. Do an ECG and other tests, I will come to see him day after tomorrow.

Bhupen: Do I have to take medicine or injections?

Doctor: I have to make your file look authentic. They will put a catheter for saline. You must lie down or else these people will start wondering whether you are a real patient or not.

Bhupen: Okay, sir, thank you.

Once we were out of the doctor's cabin, Dalvi told us about the admission procedure and about how a patient was taken for MRI and minor tests. We thanked him and he replied saying he always handled such cases well.

Dalvi: You saw my relations with the doctor; now you are admitted.

Bhupen: Should I give the money now?

Dalvi: How much is it?

Bhupen: Rs 15,000.

Dalvi then took us to a remote place and pocketed the cash.

Dalvi: Fill the form now. I will just meet the doctor and come back.

Bhupen: Thank you. In which ward will I be kept?

Dalvi: Ward number 8. And the medicine which they give you, throw it away.

In just a few minutes, I was taken to a special room, which had an attached toilet and bathroom. Though the room was filthy, I was better off than the other patients in cramped wards. The city's biggest government hospital, which is always 'full' for people coming in from remote corners of the state, is more than open for those who shell out money to prevent getting caught. During the few hours I spent there, I was examined by some of the nurses on duty. They took my ECG and tried to determine why I was having chest pain. I feared further treatment. I didn't want to take the medicines they gave me fearing they might cause health problems. Also, lying on the hospital bed doing nothing added to the fear and tension.

After the admission formalities were completed, I asked Priti to coordinate with a staff photographer who would click photos of me on the hospital bed in the patient clothes they had given me to wear as evidence for my story. One of the paper's brightest photographers, Sachin, was assigned to the task. Priti helped him sneak into the ward. Sachin stayed by my side, pretending to be my relative.

Escape from the Hospital

Dressed in a white kurta and pyjama given by the hospital, I waited for the right moment. It was important for me to gather as much evidence as possible before leaving. After the photographs were clicked, I focused on getting my hands on medical papers signed by the doctor. I asked the nurse on duty to get my papers on the pretext of checking the medicines.

After taking a round of the hospital, I realized that the morning shift was soon coming to an end and a new set of ward boys and peons would be taking charge. This was the ideal time to plan my escape. A few minutes before the shift ended, the staff at the hospital headed to the changing rooms to change out of their uniforms before leaving for the day. The staff on the next shift wouldn't recognize me and if I managed to change out of my patient clothes, I could easily escape. Just before the shift was about to end, I asked Sachin to wait outside the hospital gate and keep his bike ready.

Priti stood outside the special ward and kept an eye on the staff till I changed. The moment I was done, I handed over the medical papers to Priti and asked her to run down and take a cab that Sachin had kept waiting outside the gate. Meanwhile, I called up Sachin and informed him that I was on my way. I panicked when I peeped out of my ward and saw the doctor who had admitted me on rounds.

He had started examining the patients one by one and was slowly moving towards my room. I rushed back in and changed into the clothes the hospital had given me. I tried calling Priti so that she could bring back the papers. Unfortunately, I could not get through to her. Despite it being January, my shirt was soaked through with sweat. I kept trying her phone but there was no response; she had probably already left for the office.

The doctor had just two more patients to see before me and one of them was in a deep slumber, so he skipped that patient. I decided that was my best option too. I pretended to be asleep as he neared my room. The idea worked, as the doctor saw me sleeping and was about to walk away when my phone started ringing. The doctor turned towards me once again. He walked towards my bed, touched my shoulder and said, 'Arey bhai, tera phone baj raha hai' (Brother, your phone is ringing). I lay still for a moment and eventually got up, rubbing my eyes. To avoid questions from the doctor, I picked up the call and heard Sachin ask me what was going on. When I didn't give him a clear answer, he realized that something was amiss, and informed me that he would wait for me downstairs. The doctor stood for a while in front of me and then walked out of my room, without saying much. Without wasting a single minute, I made a second attempt to escape. I changed my clothes again and ran out of the ward, heading straight for the exit. I even heard someone calling out to me from behind, but I did not stop. I saw Sachin waiting on his bike and we sped away. I had been admitted at 12.20 p.m. and had managed to stay in the ward for five hours.

Within hours of the *Mumbai Mirror*'s story on the doctor–criminal nexus at the state-run J.J. Hospital, the state Medical Education Department instituted an inquiry. The committee—comprising a joint director-level officer from the Medical Education Department and two senior professors from J.J. Hospital—questioned all the ward boys and doctors mentioned in the story on 19 January 2008 and recorded their statements. The state government took serious note of the incident and appointed a committee to investigate.

The doctor who was incriminated by our report, who headed the medicine department and admitted me to the hospital, claimed in his statement that I had said I had financial problems because of which I suffered from stress and chest pain. However, a transcript of the conversation between the doctor and me clearly proved that no such thing was discussed.

The doctor had also said that I did not want any needle pricks, but that was not possible and an intravenous injection had to be given in case of an emergency to administer medicines.

He said all this without ascertaining what was wrong with a perfectly fit person. But in any case, as per the conversation recorded by us, the doctor was heard saying that a few needle pricks would help me strengthen my case and stay in hospital a little longer.

In his statement, the doctor also said that he had never met me and did not accept any money from me. He added that he could not be held accountable for transactions that took place when he wasn't present.

Mumbai Mirror, in its report, had clearly mentioned that none of the doctors accepted money themselves, but the transcripts clearly pointed to monetary benefits for the doctor, especially as I was admitted without any prior check-up.

After facing the inquiry panel, the doctor even visited our office, demanding to see the evidence. Justifying his actions, the doctor said, 'The ward boy told me that Bhupen was his brother, and that he had chest pain. He pleaded with me to get him admitted, so I did the needful.' Eventually the inquiry against the doctor met the same fate as other cases. Other doctors protected him and ensured his name was eventually cleared. One of them even filed a suit against us but his charges were never proved in the court of law.